The Remaking of the British Working Class, 1840–1940

HISTORICAL CONNECTIONS

Series editors
Tom Scott, University of Liverpool
Geoffrey Crossick, University of Essex
John Davis, University of Connecticut
Joanna Innes, Somerville College, University of Oxford

Titles in the series

The Decline of Industrial Britain
Michael Dintenfass

The French Revolution
Gwynne Lewis

The Italian Risorgimento
Lucy Riall

The Rise of Regional Europe
Christopher Harvie

Medicine in the Making of Modern Britain, 1700–1920
Christopher Lawrence

Forthcoming titles

Catholic Politics in Europe 1918–1945
Martin Conway

Environment and History
William Beinart and Peter Coates

Fascism in Italy and Germany
Alex de Grand

Nationalism in the USSR
Stephen Jones

Popular Politics in Nineteenth-Century England
Rohan McWilliam

Population Policies in Twentieth-Century Dictatorships and Democracies
Maria Quine

The Unification of Germany
Michael John

The Remaking of the British Working Class, 1840–1940

Mike Savage and Andrew Miles

ROUTLEDGE

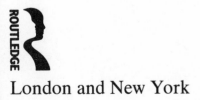

London and New York

First published 1994
by Routledge
11 New Fetter Lane, London EC4P 4EE

Simultaneously published in the USA and Canada
by Routledge
29 West 35th Street, New York, NY 10001

© 1994 Mike Savage and Andrew Miles

Typeset by Computerset, Harmondsworth, Middlesex
Printed in Great Britain by Redwood Books, Trowbridge, Wiltshire

British Library Cataloguing in Publication Data
A catalogue record for this book is available from the British
Library.

Library of Congress Cataloging in Publication Data
Savage, Michael.
    The remaking of the British working class, 1840–
1940/   Mike Savage and Andrew Miles.
       p. cm. – (Historical connections)
    Includes bibliographical references and index.
       1. Working class–Great Britain–History–19th century.
2. Working class–Great Britain–History–20th century.   I.
Miles. Andrew. 1961–   . II. Title. III. Series.
HD8390.S28   1994
305.5'.62'0941–dc20
93–38448

ISBN 0-415-07320-0

Contents

Tables and figures

Series editors' preface

Historical Connections is a new series of short books on important historical topics and debates, written primarily for those stydying and teaching history. The books will offer original and challenging works of synthesis that will make new themes accessible, or old themes accessible in new ways, build bridges between different chronological periods and different historical debates, and encourage comparative discussion in history.

If the study of history is to remain exciting and creative, then the tendency to fragmentation must be resisted. The inflexibility of older assumptions about the relationship between economic, social, cultural and political history has been exposed by recent historical writing, but the impression has sometimes been left that history is little more than a chapter of accidents. This series will insist on the importance of processes of historical change, and it will explore the connections within history: connections between different layers and forms of historical experience, as well as connections that resist the fragmentary consequences of new forms of specialism in historical research.

Historical Connections will put the search for these connections back at the top of the agenda by exploring new ways of uniting the different strands of historical experience, and by affirming the importance of studying change and movement in history.

Geoffrey Crossick
John Davis
Joanna Innes
Tom Scott

Introduction and acknowledgements

The study of class has never been dispassionate. Histories of the working class are not detached studies of how manual workers lived in previous generations, even if they present themselves as such. They are also political documents. They contain implicit, and sometimes explicit, ideas about social and political change which can only be understood in the context of historians' own beliefs about the nature of class divisions and hopes for political change.

As we explain in Chapter 1, in the past decade working-class history has been written in an intellectual and political climate in which the significance of class itself has been called into question. Some historians have become doubtful of the historical importance of social class, and question its salience for working people in the past. As a result, historical studies of the working class, which flourished only a decade ago, are in a state of considerable uncertainty. It has become increasingly unclear what the point of working-class history is, if class seems to mean so little to people, whether in the past or the present.

Our book is designed to introduce these historical debates to students and other interested readers. But it is also a book with an argument. Its specific aim is to defend a sophisticated approach to class analysis in historical research. While we acknowledge the force of recent critiques of class, we show that studies of class formation can be adapted to meet them. More specifically we show how a complex but nonetheless distinct process of 'working-class formation' took place in British society between 1840 and 1940, which we argue had major political implications. Our aim is to put class analysis firmly back on the historical agenda.

The structure of the book has been devised to develop an argument chapter by chapter. Although individual chapters can be consulted for specific issues, they frequently take up points introduced in earlier ones. Chapter 1 provides a brief survey of how the history of the working class is rewritten in different periods following the changing political context. It relates the current unpopularity of the concept of class to current developments in British (and world) politics. Further, it advances the rudiments of a more adequate approach to social class. Some readers may find it frustrating that Chapter 1 avoids discussing the empirical material used by various historians to marshal their arguments. But this is deliberate. Our intention is to show that histories of the working class are not disinterested pieces of research which should only be evaluated against the historical 'evidence': they also need to be understood in relation to the political context in which they were written.

Chapters 2, 3 and 4 each examine a separate area of working-class formation. Chapter 2 shows that the male working class was becoming more homogeneous in the years after 1840, and in particular how entrenched divisions between skilled and unskilled workers lost their salience. Chapter 2 also points out that the position of women was rather different from that of men and that they came to occupy a much more ambiguous class position. Chapter 3 examines the changing nature of work relations, and argues that while changes in the work process itself were not especially dramatic, the labour market was subject to bureaucratic pressures which threatened the position of skilled male workers. Chapter 4 explores the urban dimension of class formation, arguing that between 1840 and 1940 urban space shifted from being largely a middle-class domain to being a working-class one.

The implications of these developments for understanding social conflict and political change are spelled out in Chapter 5, which brings together the arguments of the book. Chapter 5 argues against the current view that the rise of the Labour Party was related to political changes alone. We show that the history of the Labour Party was shaped in complex ways by the processes of class formation discussed in previous chapters. While the strategies, policies and ideas of the party cannot be reduced to these developments, they provide a vital context for explaining the fortunes of the Labour movement.

Many people have helped us in the course of writing this book. Our particular thanks go to the editorial team of the Historical Connections series for inviting us to contribute. Jo Innes and especially Geoff Crossick have given us very helpful comments and advice on various drafts. Thanks also to Helen Hills, Nev Kirk and John Seed for their comments on previous drafts; to John Goldthorpe and Clive Payne for their interest and advice at various stages of the research on social mobility; to Len Schwarz for his spreadsheet skills; and to Sue Kennedy for her secretarial support. Various parts of this book have benefited from seminar discussions. Parts of Chapter 2 were first introduced by Andrew Miles at the Economic History Conference (April 1989), and subsequently in papers presented to economic history seminars at Oxford and Bristol Universities. The ideas in Chapter 4 had a preliminary airing in a seminar organised by R. J. Morris on 'New Directions in Urban History' at the University of Essex in September 1992, and in a seminar at Manchester Metropolitan University in April 1993.

Finally, it should be noted that we have found it difficult to resolve the apparently perennial problem of whether to refer to 'our' working class as British or English. While all of the data in Chapter 2 exclude Scotland, some include Wales. However, we do refer to Scottish research in Chapters 3, 4 and 5. There are also large parts of England which we have not had space to discuss fully. Therefore people must make up their own minds as to whether we are justified in finally deciding to call our book *The Remaking of the* British *Working Class.*

Mike Savage and Andrew Miles
Keele and Birmingham
September 1993

1 Politics and the British working class

The fundamental question which lies behind working-class history is that of agency. To what extent, in what form and for what reasons do workers become politically active and so affect historical developments? This chapter shows how answers to this question have changed according to the political climate in which historians were working. In particular it distinguishes three different perspectives on working-class history which have gained prominence at various times. First, early historical research optimistically believed that working-class agency was steadily increasing as the influence of the institutions of the Labour movement – trade unions, the Labour Party, the co-operative societies – grew. 'Labour history' was the history designed to service and celebrate the Labour movement. Second, from the 1950s and 1960s a new form of working-class social history began to develop which was more critical of the Labour movement, and denied that it was the necessary or inevitable form of working-class politics. Instead, this new social history located working-class agency in the activities of workers in their workplaces, in their homes and in their leisure activities. It sought 'real' working-class agency in the routines and practices of everyday life, away from the terrain of bureaucratic party politics. Third, since the mid-1970s, partly as a result of the electoral weakness of the Labour Party, there has been greater questioning about whether the working class has ever been an important historical agent. The result has been a new form of historical research which downplays the importance of class and rereads the historical record to bring out the importance of non-class forms of agency.

This chapter discusses the basic features of each approach, and argues that the recent reappraisal of class, while a helpful critique of earlier simplistic theories, need not invalidate a reformulated perspective which we term the class formation paradigm. We briefly elaborate this perspective as an introduction to the chapters which follow.

LABOUR HISTORY

In the years between 1945 and 1960 social class seemed the fundamental division in British society. The working class held a particularly visible place within this system. In the 1950s manual workers comprised no less than 70 per cent of the workforce, and the Labour Party and trade union movement enjoyed unprecedented popularity. The Labour movement was a magnet for all 'progressive' thought, and seemed to be the main force driving economic and social progress. The first majority Labour government, led by Clement Attlee and elected by a landslide in 1945, considerably expanded the provision of public welfare, and nationalised a significant sector of the economy. Although Labour lost power in 1951, the Conservatives made little attempt to undo its reforms.

In this climate labour history, the celebration of this new, powerful political movement, came of age. Labour historians examined the history of the Labour movement, its origins in early English radicalism of the eighteenth and nineteenth centuries, and traced the development of working-class organisations (Webb and Webb 1902; Cole 1948). Particular attention was paid to the emergence of trade unionism, and the development of the Labour Party itself from the 1890s (e.g. Pelling 1965; Bealey and Pelling 1958). Labour historians tended to adopt an evolutionary perspective, in which early, rudimentary forms of worker organisation were inevitably replaced by more institutional, effective ones. Labour historians were not interested in political or cultural forms which did not appear to prefigure the twentieth century Labour movement, with the result that a variety of popular movements such as millenarian religion, producer co-operation, early feminist movements, self-help medical clubs or working-class Conservatism had little place in their histories. More generally, there was little interest in those many areas of working-class life which were not associated in some way with the Labour movement.

Over the course of the 1950s and the early 1960s the perspective of labour history matured. It became less concerned with simply charting the chronology of the rise of the Labour movement – a project which the Webbs and G.D.H. Cole had pioneered in the early twentieth century. Trade union histories became sophisticated exercises, increasingly written by academics (e.g. Musson 1954; Bagwell 1963). Admittedly, labour history struggled to get full recognition in more conservative history departments, but it had emerged as a legitimate form of historical inquiry. Perhaps the single most important historian in developing labour history, but also in challenging some of its ideas and preconceptions, was Eric Hobsbawm.

Hobsbawm's work, which began to appear in articles written in the later 1940s and 1950s (collected in Hobsbawm 1964), was distinctive due to his ambivalence towards the Labour movement. Because he was a Communist, he tended to see the rise of Labour not as a progressive political development, but rather as one which allowed the consolidation of capitalism through its reluctance to countenance revolutionary politics. Hobsbawm's interest lay not in charting the rise of the Labour movement, but in explaining why its 'reformist' politics had come to prevail over other political movements within the working class. Hobsbawm also set about exploring the puzzling time-lag between the development of the working class brought about by industrialisation from the late eighteenth century, and the emergence of the modern Labour movement which did not occur until the late nineteenth century.

Hobsbawm explained this time-lag in two ways, both of which were to have a deep influence on later debates. The first of these stressed how long it took for industrial workers to become familiar with the cultural norms of the new industrial-capitalist society. In the early nineteenth century workers were still governed by preindustrial values, with the result that it took them many years to come to terms with the logic and demands of industrial capitalism. In the early stages of industrialisation, skilled workers could have demanded a higher wage than they actually got, such was the scarcity of their skills, but they did not think of doing so since they were used to getting what they regarded as the customary rate for the job. The process by which workers came to learn the new 'rules of the game', in which they accepted that their wages were to be regulated by the laws of supply and demand, was a long one.

Hobsbawm claimed that change began in the 1840s, when trade unions started to recognise the importance of the trade cycle and to provide benefits for the unemployed. However, the idea of the 'fair day's wage' still persisted, and it was not until the 1890s that workers began to adjust their sights. Only at this point did they accept that their wages should reflect market conditions rather than the intrinsic skill of a particular job, and learn to adapt to the trade cycle, taking what advantage they could when employment was relatively full.

Thus Hobsbawm could explain both how a reformist Labour Party became the 'natural' party of the working class, and why it took so long to do so. However, subsequent historiography was more influenced by Hobsbawm's second explanation of the time-lag: the idea, borrowed, in fact, from the thoughts of Engels and Lenin, of the 'labour aristocracy'. This theory tried to explain the hiatus between the decline of

early radicalism after 1850 and the development of the Labour movement after 1880 in terms of the existence of a distinct worker 'elite',
with superior earnings and work conditions, living separate from the
mass of the working class. Quiescent while in possession of a distinct
set of economic and social privileges from the mid-nineteenth century,
this stratum, he argued, was repoliticised by the attack on it after
1880.

Hobsbawm's work was vital in shifting interest away from labour
institutions alone to the wider economic, social and cultural forces
which shaped them. His work paved the way for historical studies of
the working class which were much more interested in a wider working-
class social history. This was particularly true in the work he inspired
on the existence of a labour aristocracy, and on the history of industrial
relations. But this reorientation was also related to political developments in the 1960s.

THE SOCIAL HISTORY OF CLASS

In the 1960s the assumption that the Labour movement was 'progressive' was put into question. A new scepticism about the achievements
of the post-war Labour movement appeared. Some socialists emphasised the limited impact of the Labour movement on British society.
One of the earliest examples of this changed sentiment was the
sociological study *Coal is Our Life*, published in 1956 (Dennis *et al.*
1969). This study was concerned with the impact of nationalisation on
coal miners, and whether the reforms of the Labour government had
changed the lives and aspirations of the miners themselves. But the
study showed that even in this supposed new era, class divisions were
little changed. Far from the Labour reforms creating a new social order
in which miners might feel they 'belonged', research showed that there
was actually a deep sense of fatalism and pessimism among them. They
were oppositional and antagonistic to management, and to the privileged in society generally. They expressed a keen awareness of class
divisions and inequalities, yet at the same time they lacked a wider
political radicalism which sought to replace existing social relations
with better ones:

> That workers in all industries do see management or employers as
> opponents cannot be doubted. . . . For the most part, however,
> workers have learned the lesson of their own history, that business is
> business. They see it as natural that the employer wishes to make a
> profit out of their work. . . . But their aim is also to make money,

and for this reason their relationship with the employer is one of
struggle for the division of the spoils.

(Dennis *et al*. 1969: 32)

Furthermore, the relationship between the Labour movement and the
working class seemed more fraught and uneasy than had been assumed
within mainstream labour history. The authors of *Coal is Our Life*
showed how shallow were the roots of the Labour Party, even in an
apparently cohesive working-class community. Although electoral
support for the Labour Party was very strong, actual political campaigning was minimal, and the Labour Party had little real cultural
presence in the life of the miners. Instead, miners tended to compen-
sate for the danger and insecurity of their work by engaging in a
hedonistic social life.

Not only was the rootedness of the Labour Party in working-class
life and culture open to question. The 'progressive' record of the
Labour Party itself was challenged. Far from ushering in real social
change, it seemed that the Labour Party had merely helped to construct a form of welfare capitalism which had done little to challenge
entrenched class divisions. This view was supported by sociological
research in the 1960s and 1970s. The continued existence of poverty
was pointed out by Abel-Smith and Townsend (1965), while Goldthorpe and Lockwood (1969) showed that even affluent workers had
no real commitment to the social order. Goldthorpe's later work (1980)
also demonstrated the very real disadvantages which working-class
children had in getting on, compared to middle-class children. New
types of social movements, for instance feminism, the gay movement
and the student movement, began to raise demands which the Labour
movement had done little to meet.

Particularly important here was the rise of the 'New Left', socialists
who saw the Labour Party as a reformist, compromised political force,
and looked to the renewal of Marxist politics. Marxists believe that the
working class is the revolutionary class – the only social group able to
overthrow capitalism and replace it with a just, Communist, society.
Socialism could not be achieved by middle-class intellectuals legis-
lating it into existence: it is only when the working class itself seizes
power that real change can come about.

The problem for Marxist writers lay in explaining why it was that the
British working class appeared more interested in going to the pub or
winning the football pools than in setting up barricades and seizing
political power. Why, despite the apparent solidarity and cohesiveness
of working-class culture, despite the unique resilience and strength of
the trade union movement, despite the entrenched class awareness

evident in British society, was the working class apparently so unwilling to engage in radical political action to achieve a better society?

Some Marxists claimed that the problem lay in the leadership of the working class. In his book *Parliamentary Socialism*, Ralph Miliband (1961) argued that the leaders of the Labour Party had systematically marginalised socialist politics throughout the twentieth century. The implication was that the working class itself actually wanted a more radical Labour Party and supported socialist politics, but that they were let down by the generally reformist, often middle-class, leadership.

The feeling that the Labour movement's leaders did not reflect popular aspirations led historians away from labour history. Instead socialist historians sought out a more radical working class elsewhere, which found expression primarily outside the Labour movement. This reorientation involved showing that the Labour movement itself was not a necessary, inevitable development, but a distortion of other, more challenging forms of working-class politics. In this way socialists could continue to proclaim the revolutionary potential of the working class even though any actual signs of such sentiment might currently be lacking. Radical historians searched for the historical traces of a genuinely oppositional working class which had been undermined by the rise of Labour.

It was this context which explains the appeal of E.P. Thompson's *The Making of the English Working Class* (first published in 1963), one of the most influential works of English social history ever written. This book rejected the idea that the English working class was politically immature or passive. Thompson argued that at the end of the eighteenth and in the early nineteenth centuries working men 'learned to see their own lives as part of a general history of conflict between the loosely defined "industrious classes" on the one hand and the unreformed House of Commons on the other' (Thompson 1968: 782). The working class led the early radical movement demanding political reform, produced a powerful critique of political corruption and injustice, and was the most important political force pressing for the creation of a democratic polity. It was the working class which was the main carrier of democratic traditions in Britain.

Thompson did not write a standard labour history because he located political radicalism in cultural forms, in communities, workplaces and social networks, rather than in bureaucratic models alone. Thus his story ended before the Chartist movement of the later 1830s and 1840s, which was in some ways the first organised political movement. Thompson's views were controversial. Two young Marxist writers, Perry Anderson and Tom Nairn, wrote a series of essays in the early 1960s which disputed Thompson's 'heroic' interpretation of the early working class. They agreed that there had been a radical moment in working-class history in the years before 1850, as Thompson suggested, but questioned its long-term significance. Nairn (1964a) argued that this early radicalism was only a series of 'revolts', forced upon workers by the desperate economic conditions under which they found themselves. As soon as these improved, as they did after 1950, it was inevitable that radicalism would wane. The workers had no developed theoretical understanding of social and political inequalities, their main targets were therefore unfocused, and they simply concentrated on gaining a place for themselves in the new social order. The decline of radicalism after 1850 was an inevitable product of the movement's earlier weaknesses.

Nairn (1964a and b) and Anderson (1963) claimed that the working class in Britain was unrevolutionary (compared to, say, the French working class) because of the long-term course of British history. They argued that Britain had never had a real bourgeois revolution, sweeping the monarchy and the aristocracy from power (in the way that the French had in 1789). This had left the emergent British working class devoid of revolutionary tradition and tutelage. The aristocracy had adapted to the development of capitalism, and their dominance prevented the conflict between capital and labour assuming the centrality it would otherwise have had.

The extensive debate provoked by these writers raises issues about the whole course of British history which go beyond the scope of this book. For our purposes it is important only to note that Thompson's views about the existence of a radical working class proved much more attractive to historians than did Anderson and Nairn's scepticism. Broad acceptance of Thompson's argument focused historical discussion on one question. What happened to the radical working class in the years after 1850 which made it into the reformist working class evident in the years after 1945? Thompson himself vacillated on this crucial question. *The Making of the English Working Class* ended its analysis in 1830. In a later essay, 'The Peculiarities of the English' (Thompson 1965), written as a direct critique of Anderson and Nairn's analysis, Thompson suggested two possible answers. First, he acknowledged that the defeat of Chartism marked the end of attempts to challenge industrial capitalism, and (echoing Hobsbawm's arguments about the 'rules of the game') he suggested that after a certain point workers cease to struggle for the transformation of society and attempt to secure their place within it:

For the workers, having failed to overthrow capitalist society, proceeded to warren it from end to end. This . . . is exactly the period when the characteristic class institutions of the Labour movement were built up – trade unions, trades councils, TUC, co-ops, and the rest – which have endured to this day. It was part of the logic of this new direction that each advance within the framework of capitalism simultaneously involved the working class far more deeply in the status quo.

(Thompson 1965: 343)

Yet Thompson's general sympathies led him to deny that radicalism had come to an end. He argued that a 'substantial minority tradition' of the articulate Left remained in the years after 1850 (Thompson 1965: 339), and that this exerted a significant influence on working-class politics, even after the development of the 'reformist' Labour Party. He pointed to figures such as William Morris (Thompson 1955) and Tom Maguire (Thompson 1961), both of whom were important influences in later nineteenth-century socialism. After 1920, the Communist Party, even though of marginal electoral importance, had a major impact on the Labour movement: 'Communism is inextricably part of British Labourism for close on fifty years', he stated (1965: 347).

Thompson therefore hedged his bets. He recognised that after Chartism industrial capitalism had secured its legitimacy, while pointing to the existence of a strong radical tradition which continued to resist it. What he did not fully address was whether this radical tradition had any substantive social roots, or whether it was largely confined to a small number of intellectuals and political activists. The new social history of class was in many ways an attempt to build on Thompson's work in order to provide a more systematic answer to the question of what happened to the radical working class in the years after 1850. Why had its enormous potential failed to realise itself?

Discussion centred on two possible explanations. First, Hobsbawm's labour aristocracy thesis was the subject of critical examination. John Foster (1974), Geoffrey Crossick (1978) and Robert Gray (1976) each carried out detailed local studies, of Oldham, Kentish London and Edinburgh respectively, to show how a distinct working-class elite emerged in the years after 1850, whose separation from the rank of semi- and unskilled workers had important cultural implications in inculcating ideas of respectability, and in reducing radicalism. However, by the later 1970s, the labour aristocracy thesis began to encounter severe criticism (Moorhouse 1978; Reid 1978; Gray 1981). Sceptics denied that a distinct labour aristocracy could be identified, given the variety of employment within the working class

(Harrison and Zeitlin 1985). On the other hand, the existence of a working-class elite could not really explain why the non-aristocratic workers were themselves deradicalised (Reid 1978, Gray 1981).

As a result of these problems a second 'solution' was considered. This was to take up the idea that changes in work relations had undermined the ability of workers to resist and challenge the social order. Stedman Jones (1975) developed this line of argument in a well-known critique of Foster's work, drawing upon Marx's distinction between 'formal' and 'real' control of labour. In early capitalism workers, while being wage-earning employees, still continued to have effective control over the tools of their trade and the skills of their work. As capitalism developed, however, employers attempted to increase productivity, and ultimately their profits, by reorganising working methods, often by introducing new machines, and taking from workers effective control over the work process. Stedman Jones argued that this transition from 'formal' to 'real' control took place around the middle of the nineteenth century and had a profound impact on working-class politics. Under 'formal' control workers continued to enjoy autonomy in the workplace, permitting them to sustain and nourish radical traditions, while encouraging them to battle to maintain their craft controls. By contrast, the real subordination of labour depoliticised the issue of worker control – since the employers had won that battle – and tended to lead to wage conflict, which was more likely to divide workers among themselves. These views were developed by Joyce (1980) who argued that after 1850 Lancashire cotton workers were deradicalised as they lost control over their work and became dependent upon their employers. This view also gained credibility due to the publication of Braverman's book, *Labour and Monopoly Capital* (1974), which also argued that capitalism tended progressively to 'deskill' workers as it sought to enhance productivity by reorganising the labour process.

Stedman Jones's views led to considerable debate, and inspired a wave of new research on the social history of work relations. Much of this suggested that workers were able to retain much more control over the work process than suggested by Stedman Jones or Joyce, and that it was therefore wrong to claim that 'real' control had been established in the mid-nineteenth century (Price 1980; Kirk 1985; Gray 1981; Zeitlin 1979; Lazonick 1979). Broadly speaking, however, it was possible to distinguish two types of critique. Some historians, such as Price (1980, 1985, 1986) and Burgess (1980) argued that Stedman Jones and Braverman were correct about the tendency for capitalism to undermine workers' skills, but disputed Stedman Jones's claim that mid-century was the critical period in which this occurred. Instead, they claimed that the period sparked off by the 'Great Depression' in 1873 saw employers make much more serious attempts to wrest work control from the hands of labour as profitability was squeezed. This interpretation made it possible to tie changes in working relations to the rise of trade unionism among semi-skilled workers, in a way which Hobsbawm (1964) had hinted was possible many years earlier. Although it offered little by way of explanation for the time-lag, Burgess (1985) and Price (1986), were able to extend this approach to argue that the rise of the Labour movement itself from the end of the nineteenth century could be related to changes in the workplace brought about by the need for employers to restructure the work process.

Other historians, however, notably Zeitlin (1985) and Reid (1985) mounted a more fundamental critique of Stedman Jones's view. They claimed that it was not simply his timing which was askew, but the very assumption that capitalism depended on undermining workers' control at all. They argued against Braverman that there is no necessary tendency for 'deskilling' to occur and argued that even after 1914 it was possible to find workers' control being reconstructed around new jobs and occupations. It was therefore fundamentally misguided to claim that 'formal' control ever gave way to 'real' control through any evolutionary process.

These issues will be taken up in greater detail in Chapter 3. Suffice it to say here that the position taken by Zeitlin and Reid emphasised that since no significant changes occurred in the workplace, historians needed to look elsewhere, for example to cultural or political change, in order to explain historical shifts in working-class politics. And indeed it was explanations of this type which were to become more prominent in the course of the 1980s. Once again, the changing political climate played a vital role in redirecting attention.

THE TURN AGAINST SOCIAL CLASS

In his Introduction to a book entitled *Labour and Socialism*, published in 1983, James Hinton struck a pessimistic note.

> When I first thought about writing [this] history ten years ago there was reason to believe that the labour movement, after a period of crisis, was poised on the brink of a great leap forward. . . . This no longer seems the right perspective. What we had thought of as the 'labour movement' has itself entered terminal crisis.
>
> (Hinton 1983: ix)

Before the 1980s nearly all studies of the working class were conducted in the shadow of the Labour movement. They supported it or they criticised it, but they did not doubt that the Labour Party, and the Labour movement more generally, represented the principal channel through which working-class political aspirations flowed or had been made to flow. In the course of the 1980s, however, this assumption came to look increasingly out of date as considerable numbers of workers appeared to abandon the Labour movement and throw in their political lot with the Conservative and centre parties.

The main catalyst was the emergence of a radical Conservative government and the apparent inability of the Labour movement to challenge it. The Labour movement itself seemed to be of declining significance. The last Labour government was elected in 1974, and in 1983 its vote fell to only 28 per cent. Although it recovered slightly from this low point, it did not rise to a level suggesting that it could reach the support it had gained in the 1940s, and in much of the south-east of England and in rural areas it became the third party behind the Liberals (later Liberal Democrats). The Labour Party no longer seemed to be a progressive force able to set the political agenda. After the defeat of radical Labour councils, notably the Greater London Council in the early 1980s, all the radical initiatives for reform seemed to come from the Conservative Party, leaving Labour as the party defending the status quo.

These political developments were themselves related to social changes which pointed to the decline of the working class. The number of manual workers began to fall from the 1960s, dropping exceptionally rapidly from the mid-1970s. Eight and a half million were employed in manufacturing in 1966, but only just over five million by 1986 (Abercrombie and Warde 1986: 82). The decline was particularly sharp in the traditional industries where working-class identities were marked. The number of miners – in some ways the archetypal working-class group – fell from around 600,000 in the later 1940s to 200,000 in the early 1980s and a mere 30,000 by the early 1990s (by which point there were more university lecturers than miners!). The defeat of the coal miners' strike in 1984/85 also seemed symptomatic of the wider failure of older forms of labour resistance.

More generally social class itself seemed less pervasive and important. Sociologists such as Pahl (1984) and Saunders (1990) argued that the working class was itself dividing into different groups. At one extreme lay a group of affluent workers, in full-time jobs, who owned their own houses and were relatively well-off. At the other extreme were those people almost permanently unemployed and confined to bad-quality rented housing (see the discussion in Gallie 1988). The former had swung to support the Conservatives in large numbers, and while the latter still tended to vote Labour, they were only a minority of the population and could therefore not play a decisive role in electing a Labour government. Some sociologists began to talk about the development of an 'underclass' separate from the rest of the working class (Saunders 1990).

The rout of traditional left-wing politics, set against the background of such ominous sociological trends, prompted radical historians to search for alternative bases of social resistance to that of class. This was a far-reaching soul-searching exercise. One of its most important aspects was a re-evaluation of the importance of culture as a vital political terrain. The social historians of class had seen cultural factors as the product of economic and social change, not themselves the arena in which political battles were fought out. This was true even when relatively sophisticated analyses of working-class culture were developed. A good example of this was Stedman Jones's article on the remaking of the London working class (1974), which complemented his analysis of changing work relations discussed above (p. 9). Stedman Jones argued that the years between 1870 and 1900 saw a fundamental remaking of working-class culture which deradicalised the working class and prepared the way for the reformist Labour movement. He argued that these years saw the emergence of a more pragmatic acceptance of the status quo among the working class:

> the most prominent developments in working class life in late Victorian and Edwardian London were the decay of artisan radicalism, the marginal impact of socialism, the largely passive acceptance of imperialism and the throne, and the growing usurpation of political and educational interests by a way of life centred round the pub, race course and music hall.
>
> (Stedman Jones 1974: 484)

Stedman Jones argued that the cultural 'remaking' of Thompson's radical working class into the more reformist version revealed in *Coal is Our Life* was a complex one, with a number of causes. He noted that by this period many of the attempts by the middle and upper classes to 'civilise' the working classes had failed. The working class rarely attended church, and ignored the range of educational and improving initiatives aimed at them in the hope of making them more 'respectable'. The important point, however, is that Stedman Jones finally explained these cultural shifts in terms of economic and social causes. He pointed to the decline of traditional artisan industries which had previously sustained a strong radical culture. He observed the rise of new semi-skilled factory work which offered workers less independence than the old crafts, and the rise of commuting which made it difficult for work traditions to spill over into neighbourhood activity. He also commented on how the introduction of compulsory elementary education from 1880 depoliticised learning processes. In short, although his focus was squarely on cultural change, he tended to see it as the product of economic and social developments.

This 'reductionist' approach to culture looked increasingly outdated in a political context in which it was the cultural victories of the Conservatives which seemed to pave the way for political, economic, and social change, rather than vice versa. Socialists such as Stuart Hall (1983) attributed the broad electoral appeal of Mrs Thatcher's political programme to its powerful cultural resonance, which stressed the ideas of nationalism, independence, and law and order.

This interest in the irreducibility of cultural phenomena to economic and social change was also related to a crisis in Marxist thought. The 'base/superstructure' metaphor, the Marxist idea that culture and politics ultimately have 'material' foundations and can therefore be explained in terms of economic change, looked increasingly difficult to defend. New intellectual currents, loosely linked to poststructuralism (e.g. Dews 1987), argued that theories like Marxism which claimed to reveal long-term historical processes were highly suspect.

The concept of class was especially prone to such a critique. Sociologists such as Hindess (1987) and Lockwood (1988) argued that the concept of class was reductionist. They claimed that the attempt by writers, particularly those of a Marxist persuasion, to explain attitudes, beliefs and behaviour simply in terms of the class location of the people concerned was misleadingly crude. The idea of class did not seem to appreciate that people actually had choices as to how they identified themselves and lived their lives, and that class might only be one, relatively unimportant, form of self-expression which people chose to adopt.

The new focus on textual meaning also led to a new scepticism about mainstream accounts of working-class culture. Books such as *Coal is Our Life*, which appeared to propound an objective account of a working-class community, were read in a different way – as partial, biased studies which were both influenced by, and helped further to construct, a particular image of the working class. This image, sometimes summarised in the descriptive title 'traditional working class' (Hobsbawm 1984), was based upon the portrayal of working-class life as standardised and homogeneous when in fact, according to the critics, the pattern of life in such communities was a good deal more complex (Davies 1992). The idea of the cosy cohesive working-class community, as served up for popular consumption in TV programmes like *Coronation Street*, could be seen not as the literal truth, but as a particular construction, created by intellectuals viewing the working class from a distance. It is, indeed, remarkable just how many of our ideas of the working class are shaped by semi-autobiographical accounts (for instance Hoggart 1957; Roberts 1973). These were frequently written by academics from working-class backgrounds who possibly romanticised working-class life and solidarity. In this way, the working class became the repository for all sorts of middle-class hopes and aspirations, perhaps with the result that historical analyses of the working class should be taken with a pinch of salt.

Research in the 1980s was certainly important in stripping away these romantic notions of working-class life. Feminist historians revealed the embedded sexism of working-class men. It was shown that working-class men had been responsible for silencing and undermining women's activity in the labour market. Taylor (1983), Cockburn (1980) and Braybon (1980), among others, all showed how male trade unionists had opposed the right of women to gain employment. Feminists also showed that the working class was deeply divided by gender, with the result that it became difficult to talk about a unitary 'working class'. Ross (1983), Roberts (1984) and Chinn (1988) emphasised women's informal power in the home and neighbourhood. And it was also shown that working-class women often engaged in political activity independent of men. Liddington and Norris (1978), for example, showed that working women had played a much larger role than previously thought in the suffrage campaigns of the late nineteenth and early twentieth centuries, and the role of women in early radical agitation such as Chartism and Owenism was also revealed (Thompson 1984; Taylor 1983).

The turn away from class was dramatically confirmed as some of the leading lights of British social history staged an abrupt *volte-face* and swiftly nailed their colours to the mast of the new scepticism. Having previously argued for the importance of work relations as the basis of class formation, writers such as Gareth Stedman Jones and Patrick Joyce began to play down the significance of economic and social factors in explaining cultural and political change. Embracing the new poststructuralist concern with texts and languages, they argued that only if texts articulated a clear and explicit sense of class, and class division, in their discourse, could it be claimed that class existed in any useful or meaningful way.

This stress on language, and on the importance of class consciousness, was in some ways old hat. It was, in fact, the main focus of E.P. Thompson's argument that class 'happens when some men [*sic*], as a result of common experiences (inherited or shared), feel and articulate the identity of their interests as between themselves, and as against other men whose interests are different from (and usually opposed to) theirs' (Thompson 1968: 9–10). For Thompson, class is therefore intimately linked to class consciousness, so that when he talks of 'the making' of the English working class he looks for this in terms of the conscious values and beliefs of the workers themselves. Thompson's formulation did not specify, however, where class consciousness was to be found.

In a famous paper on Chartism, published in 1983, Stedman Jones took up the theme that to determine people's values and beliefs, greater attention should be paid to the precise language they use. In a detailed examination of Chartist writing Stedman Jones claimed that 'Chartism was a political movement and political movements cannot satisfactorily be defined in terms of the anger and disgruntlement of disaffected social groups or even the consciousness of class' (Stedman Jones 1983: 96). Chartist language made little explicit reference to economically defined classes, to groups exploited in the workplace. Rather, Chartists used a political language and saw their task as 'the ending of a monopoly situation in which all other forms of property were afforded political and legal support while that of labour was left at the mercy of those who monopolized the state and law' (Stedman Jones 1983: 109). Hence theirs was a political movement, aimed at achieving political reform of a corrupt state, and it should not be interpreted by subsequent generations of historians in terms of social class.

Patrick Joyce (1990) made an even stronger case for the importance of language. Influenced by the work of the American historian William Reddy (1987), who argued that French textile workers of the late nineteenth century did not deploy a language of class, Joyce argued that Lancashire workers used a language of class in only highly circumscribed ways. Joyce asserted that the language used in popular idioms such as dialect poetry, ballads and popular theatre did not seem to make specific reference to class divisions or inequalities. Instead, Joyce argues that a populist framework was much more common. This populist mentality did not distinguish between classes but between 'the people' in general and a corrupt governing establishment. Only after 1914, Joyce admits, might class have become culturally important.

This current of work has formed part of a major re-evaluation of the English radical tradition itself. Whereas Thompson had associated the radical tradition with working-class politics, seeming almost to legitimate the culture of radicalism by showing its close affiliation with workers, the new historians were intent on removing the class dimensions of popular radicalism. In the context of the 1960s, when class seemed of fundamental importance, Thompson's approach helped to rehabilitate an otherwise neglected radical tradition. By the 1980s, however, it seemed that there was possibly more value in ditching the class dimensions of radicalism and emphasising other aspects of its appeal. Even from the later 1970s a number of criticisms of the idea that early radicalism had a distinct class basis had begun to appear. Prothero (1979) emphasised that many early radicals saw themselves primarily as artisans. Calhoun (1982) contended that it was a movement of preindustrial communities under threat, and that it was mistaken to see it in class terms. By the mid-1980s a major rehabilitation of the radical and liberal traditions was underway. Biagini (1992) argued that the radical tradition survived the end of the Chartist movement and resurfaced in Victorian Liberalism (see also several essays in the collection edited by Biagini and Reid 1991).

This re-evaluation of the radical tradition has also led to questions being raised about the real historical importance of socialism. Whereas labour historians had regarded the absence of labour institutions as the historical anomaly which needed to be explained, revisionist historians increasingly saw socialism as the historical oddity. Historians such as McKibbin (1990) and Benson (1989) emphasised the weakness of the Labour movement, even in its apparent heyday. Between 1918 and 1945, it was the Conservatives rather than Labour who dominated the political scene. Perhaps it was only the exceptional circumstances brought about by the Second World War which gave the Labour movement a brief period of political dominance, and even then it only lasted a few years.

These arguments, taken individually, offered particular criticisms of specific historical claims. Taken together, however, they provided an influential and wide-ranging critique of the idea that the Labour movement in particular, and the working class in general, has ever been an important political agent in British history. Many historians continued to write 'traditional' labour and social history, of course, but the point of such work looked increasingly uncertain. The end result of this new revisionism was to throw into question the long-term significance of class, and to rejuvenate a form of historical analysis concerned to emphasise the contingency of historical developments. Insofar as political events are contextualised, the main point of reference is to political cultures. Attempts to relate political and cultural developments to socio-economic forces are treated with suspicion. The implications are to rehabilitate the very type of traditional political history which had been so powerfully attacked by labour historians and social historians from the 1960s.

CLASS ANALYSIS RECLAIMED

The 'deconstruction' of class has had both positive and negative effects. Positively, it has been very useful in questioning old shibboleths and recognising that there is, indeed, no automatic relationship between the social structure and political movements. As Stedman Jones has written, 'There are no simple rules of translation from the social to the political . . . the "objective" realities of class discerned by social surveys and sociological analysis do not have any unambiguous bearing upon the fate of class oriented political parties' (Stedman Jones 1983: 242). This passage correctly insists on the complexity of the connections between economic, social, cultural and political change; it recognises that these spheres do not relate together in any deterministic fashion and lays the way open for a sophisticated analysis of what are intricate historical relationships.

What is disappointing, however, is that the prominence given to language in these new accounts does not actually help to meet this need to examine these complex connections. The stress on language all too easily slides into a form of linguistic determinism, in which the historical impact of any non-linguistic realm is obscured, denied or declared unknowable. The turn against social class, in favour of a form of historical research in which only the concepts, idioms and grammars used in discourse are regarded as open to examination, is profoundly disabling, not to say misleading. Stedman Jones and Joyce do not deny the existence of class, but are prepared only to admit very special languages as languages of class. Only if people use a language which explicitly refers to economic exploitation between classes do the authors allow that they might have stumbled across class. But this is unduly restrictive. There are many sentiments and values which may express feelings relating to the existence of class divisions in an indirect or oblique way. Indeed, this is quite clear from *Coal is Our Life*.

> The working man . . . thinks not in the abstract terms of social and economic relations . . . but in a more concrete way . . . his pride in being a worker and his solidarity with other workers is a pride in the

fact that they are real men who work hard for their living.

(Dennis *et al*. 1969: 33)

To judge popular culture purely in terms of the formal structure of its discourse is actually to intellectualise it, and to subject it to fundamentally academic ways of thinking. Much of the meaning which specific texts possess depends on the contexts in which they are created and understood. If texts are used within environments powerfully structured by class there may be little point in establishing class as a salient divide discursively – it may be so obvious to people that it needs no reference in a particular text. In short, in order properly to gauge the meanings of texts for their participants it is necessary to examine how and why they were constructed, and how they are interpreted. This involves moving beyond the formal analyses of the languages they contain to the concrete social situations which mediate their production and reception.

Given this need to recognise the context in which discourses operate, it is important to note that the linguistic approach signally fails because it ends up by constructing a polarised and ultimately unbridgeable gulf between discourses and social relations. There is no good reason, however, for thinking in these terms. Rather than discourse being contrasted with material forces, or culture juxtaposed to social structures, we would insist on their inseparable and mutually dependent character. In this we follow the claims of writers such as Giddens (e.g. 1984), Abrams (1982) and Bhaskar (e.g. 1989) who stress the recursive nature of social life, the intimate association between structure and action. In Abrams's words, 'people's action is shaped by the historically given social structures within which they find themselves and . . . their action becomes a process through which those structures are in turn changed' (Abrams 1982: 14).

Therefore it is essential to retain some conception of social structures while always recognising their mutability and complexity. For the purposes of class analysis, focus should be directed to those exploitative social structures which define the antagonistic relations lying at the heart of class conflict. The centrality of capitalist social relations is of major significance here. Marxists argue that capitalism is a system which depends on the exploitation of one class by another. Workers are never paid, in their wages, the full value of the work they carry out for their employer. On the other hand, if labourers received the full value of their work employers would not be able to make profits, and so firms would not survive. The result is that even the kindest employers are forced to exploit their workers to keep their enterprise viable. However, while we believe that capitalist exploitation remains fundamental to class divisions, not everything is reducible to capitalism. There are other discrete arenas of exploitation. which may or may not interact with capitalist social relations, and these need to be studied in specific historical contexts. For instance, Wright (1985) has shown that relations of subordination between managers and workers in organisational hierarchies are not simply dependent upon capitalism. More familiarly, patriarchal gender relations can also be identified as systems in which men exploit women in various ways (e.g. Walby 1986). As we shall emphasise below, the interplay between capitalism and patriarchy is crucial to an understanding of class formation and political action.

Identifying processes of exploitation is one thing, but they do not in themselves guarantee that people will act in any particular way. As sociologists such as Wright (1985) and Goldthorpe (1980) have insisted, it is a contingent matter whether social classes are formed on the basis of these structural inequalities or not. It is necessary to examine 'how far classes have formed as relatively stable collectivities' (Goldthorpe 1984: 491). The process of class formation is not ensured by the existence of exploitative social relations, and depends on the existence of the social, cultural and political resources which might allow it to occur. In other words, there is no guarantee that classes will form, even if social inequalities are intense. Historical research is necessary to ascertain whether such class formation occurs, and if so the reasons for it.

In order to establish possible connections between exploitative social relations and class formation, it is important to recognise the interplay between what we term 'formal' and 'practical' politics (see also Savage 1987). In this chapter we have seen historians shift between a focus (as in labour history) on institutional politics organised through political parties, usually in the electoral or public arena, and what might be termed 'the politics of everyday life' (as in the social history tradition) where the routine and informal activities of people's existence are also seen as involving political choices, strategies and decisions. Personal relationships, between husbands and wives for example, can be political, as can the business of organising and participating in ostensibly non-political activities, such as religious worship, education or sport. Crucially, it must be recognised that, alongside the arena of formal politics, there is a local and more immediate realm of political activity, which is rooted in the struggles of people as they conduct their everyday lives: the realm of 'practical' politics. The connections between these two types of politics are contingent.

To develop this point, class-based political activity takes place around the strategies adopted by people, both employers and workers, to reduce the insecurities which are inherent in capitalist society. Employers reduce their insecurity by making profits, which they do by exploiting workers, paying them only the going rate, or market value, for their labour. Workers, who are dependent on wages because they have no property of any significance to fall back on, try to reduce their insecurity by circumventing the 'rules' of the market. The strategies, or practical politics, that are adopted can take a number of forms, depending on the particular mix of resources and capacities held by specific groups of workers in given local environments. So, although working-class politics can be related to specific material interests, their realisation, and the particular form they take, can, and do, vary. Moreover, practical politics has no fixed relationship with the more familiar world of formal politics. National political structures are largely autonomous, but to gain electoral support they must make their programmes relevant to the people they want to vote for them. As workers' strategies vary from place to place, this is a complicated business, and the development and articulation of programmes with which the link between parties and constituencies is forged is more often than not crucially dependent on the organisational and inter-pretative abilities of local political activists.

The framework we have developed here is designed to show how connections between diverse economic, social, cultural and political developments can be made. It is sensitive to contingency, but insists that social, cultural and political change be analysed in the broader context of class formation. We see this perspective as a development and elaboration of the type of class analysis initiated by E.P. Thompson and Eric Hobsbawm (see generally Kaye 1982). The aim of this book is to use this elaborated framework to show that in the years between 1840 and 1940 the working class did form a distinct social-class collectivity, and that this had a major impact on political alignments.

2 Occupational change, income and demographic class formation

This chapter examines the formation of the working class in the years between 1840 and 1940 as a product of the consolidation of barriers between manual workers and various middle-class groups on the one hand, and of the declining differentiation within the working class on the other. The argument is in some ways a familiar one (Hobsbawm 1964), but we intend to use new data to substantiate it, to point out various qualifications, and to identify neglected features of the process. In particular, we draw attention to the way that while men's fates became increasingly bound up with class, women's fortunes were less so, with the result that they came to occupy an ambivalent position in the class structure.

Our argument draws upon three main bodies of evidence. First, we examine occupational change, drawing attention to the heterogeneity of the working class, but also to the tendency for male manual workers to become concentrated in manufacturing, trade and transport. Second, we examine the course of income differentials between classes and within the working class, in order to show that while incomes within the manual working class tended to converge, they diverged sharply from those of expanding middle-class groups. Finally, using the recent research of Miles (1992), we examine patterns of social mobility in order to show how patterns of differentiation within the working class were substantially reduced over time.

The aim of the last part of this chapter is therefore to explore what the sociologist John Goldthorpe (1980) has referred to as 'demographic class formation'. This measures the salience of boundaries between classes in terms of the ease by which people can move between them. Demographic class formation does not necessitate class-based action, still less can the pattern of action which might result be predicted in advance. However, when it is absent, sustained collective organisation is unlikely.

OCCUPATIONAL STRUCTURE

When Marx wrote *Das Kapital* in the 1860s and 1870s he saw British industry as the harbinger of a new era, embodying new relations of exploitation between employers and workers, which were themselves the product of an unprecedented revolution in working methods and technologies. Other contemporaries felt much the same (Kumar 1978). Today, however, very little of this picture remains (though see the recent revision by Berg and Hudson 1992). Historians now tend to stress the limitations of industrialisation in Britain rather than its impact. It is the slowness and unevenness of change which commands historical attention, rather than its pace and linearity. To give a few examples: in 1911 there were more women employed as domestic servants (about 1.4 million) than there were (male) coal miners. In the same year there were still more agricultural labourers (around 1.3 million) than there were textile manufacturing workers. The industrial factory worker was far from being typical of the working class as a whole.

Table 2.1 Industrial distribution of the labour force 1871–1951 (per cent)

	1871	*1891*	*1911*	*1931*	*1951*
Agriculture	15	11	8	6	5
Mining	5	5	7	6	4
Manufacturing	33	33	33	34	39
Building	7	6	6	5	6
Trade/transport	19	23	22	22	22
Personal services	15	16	14	8	2
Professional/ administrative	6	7	8	11	15

Source: B. R. Mitchell and P. Deane (1962), *Abstract of British Historical Statistics*, Cambridge: Cambridge University Press.

The British working class has always been heterogeneous. Table 2.1 shows that no single sector of employment ever accounted for more than 40 per cent of the workforce throughout the period. Even at the peak of Britain's industrial primacy the majority of workers were not employed in manufacturing. The British working class was never purely an industrial working class. Throughout the period, in fact, a substantial minority of people continued to work in what might be termed 'traditional' sectors of employment, notably agriculture and domestic service. Here workers were likely to work closely with their employers. Employees were dispersed between villages and houses, making it difficult to form a wider solidarity with their 'brothers or sisters' (though in some agricultural communities labourers might form closer bonds, see Howkins 1981). They were often dependent on their employers for accommodation as well as work, could easily be dismissed, and because they tended to work directly alongside their masters and mistresses found it difficult to express the 'independence' typical of other workers (see Chapter 3).

That having been said, clear trends were at work which served to increase the importance of manufacturing employment for the working class. In 1871 the working class found employment in four main sectors: manufacturing (33 per cent), trade and transport (19 per cent), agriculture (15 per cent) and domestic service (15 per cent). By 1931, however, the significance of agriculture and domestic service taken together had fallen considerably, to 14 per cent, leaving manufacturing and trade and transport as by far the most important sectors of employment. Indeed, despite the decline of British industry relative to its competitors from as early as the late Victorian period (Dintenfass 1992), the share of the workforce employed in industry rose to an all time high of 39 per cent as late as 1951.

However, an important qualification is necessary here, for there were marked contrasts in the employment experience of men and women. Women were increasingly concentrated in the 'traditional' sectors, but also in newer white-collar forms of employment. Here contacts between the classes remained common, the main change being the substitution of female middle-class mistresses in domestic service for predominantly male middle-class bosses where clerical and secretarial work were concerned. The number of female clerks grew remarkably, from 179,000 in 1911 to 648,000 by 1931, and nearly 1.5 million in 1951, when this sector accounted for one in five of all working women (Routh 1980: 6, Table 1.1). Table 2.2 (Lewis 1984: 156) shows that in 1881 nearly as many women were employed in textile work as in domestic service. By 1931, the proportion of women working in textiles had almost halved, but along with the expanding white-collar sector, women were still employed in large numbers in personal service.

The concomitant of this point, of course, is that men were increasingly concentrated in those sectors of employment in which regular contact with other classes was rare. Although the number of men in white-collar employment also rose over the period, it did so much more slowly. Routh's figures suggest that in 1931 less than 6 per

Table 2.2 Occupational distribution of women, England and Wales, 1881–1951 (percentage in major occupational groups)

	1881	1891	1901	1911	1921	1931	1941	1951
Personal service	—	—	42	39	33	35	—	23
Indoor domestic	36	35	33	27	23	24	—	11
Other	—	—	9	12	10	11	—	12
Clerks, typists, etc.	—	—	1	2	8	10	—	20
Commerce and finance	—	—	7	9	10	11	—	12
Professional and technical	5	6	7	8	7	7	—	8
Textile goods and dress	18	17	16	14	11	9	—	7
Textile workers	17	15	14	13	12	10	—	6
Metal manufacturers and engineers	—	—	1	2	3	2	—	3
Shopkeepers, packers, etc.	—	—	—	—	2	3	—	3
Transport, etc.	—	—	—	—	2	3	—	3
Paper, printing	1	2	2	2	2	2	—	1
Food, drink, tobacco	—	—	1	1	2	1	—	1
Leather, fur	—	—	—	—	3	1	—	1
Agriculture	2	1	1	2	2	1	—	1
Unskilled/unspecified	—	—	—	—	1	3	—	6

Source: E. James, 'Women and Work in Twentieth Century Britain', *Manchester School of Economics and Social Science XXX* (September 1962), Figure 2, p. 291 (taken from Lewis 1984).

cent of males were clerks, while around one-seventh of men were employed in agricultural, clerical and service employment, compared to two-fifths of women (reworking of tables in Routh 1980). The male working class had become, by the inter-war years, one primarily based in the manufacturing, trade and transport sectors. The last residues of 'traditional' employment for them had virtually ended.

These trends forged a complex and interacting set of boundaries between the genders and the classes. In general, shifts in employment led to the decline of forms of work allowing ready 'inter-class' relations. However, there was an important exception to this among working-class women. The occupational world of men became more firmly class divided, while women continued to occupy a rather more shadowy, ambiguous position, thereby complicating and undermining tendencies towards social cleavage.

INCOME INEQUALITY AND LABOUR MARKET DIVISIONS

The period saw considerable shifts in the distribution of income between different occupational groups, as well as a marked improvement in real wages. Benson (1989: 55) cites an index of real wages (a calculation of income which takes the cost of living into account) which rose from a base of 100 in 1850 to 170 by 1906, 190 by 1913/14, 234 by 1924 and 354 by 1935. This is not to say that everyone gained. Especially during the inter-war period, high levels of unemployment helped to ensure the persistence of chronic poverty (Vincent 1991; Davies 1992). What is particularly important for our argument, however, is that this period saw the consolidation of income differences between the working class and the middle class at the same time that working-class incomes were converging.

Routh's (1980) thorough analysis provides comprehensive figures for income levels by using total annual earnings derived from wages censuses. The figures from individual occupations were aggregated into seven occupational classes, including skilled manual workers, semi-skilled manual workers and unskilled manual workers (see Table 2.3). Table 2.3 expresses the incomes of the seven classes in terms of their percentage of the mean income of the entire population. Any figure above 100 indicates that the group earns more than the mean, any figure below shows that the group earns below the mean. It can immediately be seen that most men have values higher than 100 and most women lower than 100, testifying to the importance of gender inequality in the labour market.

Table 2.3 Pay structure: occupational class averages as percentage of the mean for all occupational classes, men and women (pounds)

	1913–14	1922–24	1935–36	1955–56	1960	1970	1978	Multiple of 1913–14
Men								
1. Professional								
A. Higher	405	372	392	290	289	211	209	0.5
B. Lower	191	204	190	115	120	136	137	0.7
2B. Managers etc.	247	307	272	279	263	245	203	0.8
3. Clerks	122	116	119	98	97	97	93	0.8
4. Foremen	152	171	169	148	144	121	118	0.8
Manual								
5. Skilled	131	115	121	117	113	104	110	0.8
6. Semi-skilled	85	80	83	88	83	93	97	1.1
7. Unskilled	78	82	80	82	76	83	86	1.1
Men's average (current weights)	116	114	115	119	120	123	121	1.0
% mean deviation	68	73	70	48	47	35	30	

Table 2.3 continued

	1913–14	1922–24	1935–36	1955–56	1960	1970	1978	Multiple of 1913–14
Women								
1. Professional								
A. Higher	—	—	—	(218)	(217)	178	169	—
B. Lower	110	137	130	82	86	88	98	0.9
2B. Manager etc.	99	102	104	151	142	135	128	1.1
3. Clerks	56	68	64	60	61	61	69	1.2
4. Forewomen	70	98	96	90	86	73	81	1.2
Manual								
5. Skilled	54	56	53	60	56	49	57	1.1
6. Semi-skilled	62	63	62	51	48	47	59	1.0
7. Unskilled	35	47	43	40	40	44	57	1.6
Women's average (current weights)*	62	66	64	60	59	58	68	1.1
% mean deviation	31	37	38	67	67	59	43	

Source: Routh (1980), p. 124.

*The exclusion of higher professional women in 1955–56 lowers the women's average to 58 and the mean deviation to 4.3.

What Table 2.3 also reveals is that before 1914 skilled male workers enjoyed wages which lay within the same orbit as foremen, clerks and even the lower professionals. However, by the inter-war years it was clear that the economic position of all manual workers sharply diverged from the middle and upper classes. In 1913 the wages of skilled workers lay closer to the earnings of foremen than they did to unskilled manual workers, and they earned as much as two-thirds of the lower professional income. By 1922 this had all changed. The earnings of foremen were half as much again as those of the skilled workers, while lower professionals earned almost double. Only clerks lay close to the manual working class, reflecting partly the downgrading of many clerical jobs but also reflecting the fact that male clerical work was sometimes a stepping stone to a better job and therefore some clerks could hope to improve their salaries on promotion (Lockwood 1958).

By the 1920s, the wages of the skilled worker had come closer to those of the semi- and unskilled workers than to those of other social groups. This marked a fundamental shift from the Victorian period, when skilled workers enjoyed considerable economic advantages over the rest of the working class. Before 1900 some skilled workers were able to earn wages which compared favourably with the middle classes. Compositors (printing workers) on daily newspapers earned an average of £2.14s (£2.70) per week in 1906, and engine drivers, piecework riveters in shipyards and glass workers were also among the highest paid (Routh 1980: 99–100). This put them on a level with teachers, draughtsmen and many clerks, and well above those scraping a living at the bottom of the pile where there was virtually no minimum to the wages which might be paid. Female box workers in east London could earn as little as 2 shillings (10p) for a week's work, while sandwich-board men earned a shilling (5p) a day for wandering the streets (Treble 1979; see also Stedman Jones 1971). It was, however, unusual for a man's wages to fall below 10 shillings (50p) a week, while agricultural labourers, known to be the poorest of the large occupational groupings, earned around 18 shillings (90p) in 1906, perhaps a third as much as the highest-paid manual workers.

Before 1900, then, there was marked variation in economic fortunes within the working class. However, after 1870 there were clear trends towards the narrowing of such differences. This has admittedly been a subject of hot debate in recent years, since a more sceptical view which tends to stress the continuity of wage differentials over time has recently become fashionable (Routh 1980; Penn 1983; Reid 1985). Table 2.3 shows clearly, however, that the mean wages of skilled men fell relative to the population at large, while those of semi- and unskilled men stayed roughly stable. In 1913/14 skilled workers earned 68 per cent more than the unskilled, a figure which fell to 40 per cent in 1922/24 before increasing again to 51 per cent in the 1930s: a differential still well below that found in the pre-war period.

The figures for women show that the earnings of unskilled workers rose in relative terms, so that earnings differentials between groups of women workers also displayed a general tendency to decline. Women workers also began to catch up – albeit slowly – with men, so that whereas unskilled female workers only earned 45 per cent of the earnings of male unskilled workers in 1913/14, this had risen to 56 per cent by 1935/36.

In short, even though Routh himself does not emphasise the trend towards equality, his figures do indeed reveal that patterns of wage inequality within the working class were reduced. Waites (1987) has recently shown that the First World War was especially important in this regard, and that despite the impact of taxation which mainly affected the upper and middle classes, their economic advantages over workers were reinforced. While there was a slight tendency for differentials among manual workers to open again in the inter-war years, they were never restored to pre-war levels. Differentials seemed to narrow universally, between groups of men, between groups of women, and between men and women.

Before leaving this topic, there is one final problem to deal with. Aggregated occupational classes contain a variety of different jobs within them. It may be the case that the apparent trend towards equality within the working class is merely a result of shifts in the occupational composition of the different aggregated classes. New jobs created by economic change might be classified as skilled even though their wage rates are below those found among older skilled workers. In this case, their growing numerical presence might depress the average earnings of skilled workers as a whole, but this would not mean that traditional wage differentials between skilled and unskilled in the older sectors were changed. However, those studies which have examined wage rates within particular industrial sectors do, in fact, suggest that such differentials did decline significantly. A good example is in the numerically important engineering industry, where Penn (1983) shows that in 1859 the unskilled earned only 52 per cent of the wages of the skilled; by 1877 this had risen to 60 per cent, by 1918 to 75 per cent, before falling slightly to 67 per cent in 1935. Similar trends can be found in building work, on the railways, and in other sectors (Routh 1980). While skilled workers continued to enjoy higher earnings than the semi- and unskilled workers into the twentieth century, there is therefore no doubt that the scale of their advantage declined over time.

SOCIAL MOBILITY AND THE WORKING CLASS

The evidence discussed so far suggests that there were much firmer boundaries between the working and middle classes after 1900 than in the mid-Victorian period, and that barriers of internal differentiation within the working class had also declined. The question which is posed by these findings is whether this affected social mobility and allowed a process of demographic class formation to ensue.

Social mobility refers to the way in which individuals move between occupations and social classes, either in the course of their own lives (intra-generational mobility), or compared to their parents (inter-generational mobility). Sociologists have seen patterns of mobility, especially over generations, as giving valuable insights into the strength of class boundaries, since they reveal how common it is for people to move between classes (Heath 1981, provides a straightforward introduction to these issues). Historians, however, have rarely considered how an analysis of social mobility might also be used to explore the issue of class formation and social relations in the past (Miles 1993a; Savage 1994).

The main problem for historians has been the absence of reliable data. There is, however, one valuable source which can be used. Following an Act of Parliament in 1836, when couples married they and their fathers all had to sign a marriage register, and the occupations of the bridegroom, the groom's and the bride's father, and sometimes the bride, were also recorded. As a result, data on the occupations of fathers and sons can readily be assembled, and analyses of inter-generational social mobility carried out. The potential of these documents for the study of historical social mobility was recognised some time ago (Sanderson 1972; Gray 1976; Crossick 1978), but no comprehensive analysis ensued. This lack has recently been rectified by Miles, who has carried out an elaborate study of English occupational and social mobility patterns in the period 1839 to 1914 (Miles 1992). The principal source used in this work was a sample of 10,835 marriages taken from ten districts across England, which was originally collected for a study of literacy (Vincent 1989).

Miles shows that there are some problems associated with the use of marriage registers. Only rarely are brides' occupations recorded, which makes it very difficult to examine women's occupational mobility. In what follows, therefore, we initially concentrate on men before examining women's mobility towards the end of the chapter. Furthermore, around 10 per cent of men and up to 14 per cent of women never married, and the social mobility of bachelors and spinsters is therefore hidden from view. This is likely to be more of a serious problem for the analysis of women's than men's mobility, since spinsters could more easily stay in employment and have a 'career', whereas married women were frequently expected to give up such aspirations on marriage. The documents are also open to the criticism that they cannot show what happened to individuals after marriage when they might have changed their occupation. However, the age group they embrace still includes a broad, and economically crucial, sector of the population (Sewell 1985). Furthermore, only the records of Anglican churches are open to researchers, leaving out those sectors of the population who either had civil marriages or were Catholics or Nonconformists. These problems become increasingly acute in the years approaching 1914, by which time 40 per cent of the population were married outside the Anglican church, making it difficult to examine social mobility in the inter-war period. It is not clear how significant this problem is, but it is unlikely that Nonconformists or Catholics had substantially different patterns of social mobility from Anglicans. For the period 1839–1914 districts with a strong Anglican presence were chosen for analysis, so as to reduce the relevance of this problem. Unfortunately this means that the social mobility analysis only covers England. However, the districts chosen (Stoke-on-Trent, Sheffield, Dudley, Macclesfield, Lichfield, Bethnal Green, Wokingham, Nuneaton, Cleobury Mortimer and Samford) encapsulate a wide variety of economies, labour markets and settlement types.

Despite these problems it should be recognised that the marriage registers offer a remarkable opportunity to examine the broad patterns of male social mobility. Miles organised the occupational data into five social classes, adapting an existing classification framework used for census statistics in 1951. It divides the working class, made up almost exclusively of men in manual employment, into three distinct strata or sub-classes: skilled, semi-skilled and unskilled. The middle class was divided into two: a lower middle class of mostly white-collar employees and small businessmen, and then the more substantial employing and professional bourgeoisie, with the small numbers of landed and titled people who appear in the sample included with the latter.

His subsequent analysis first sheds light on the boundaries between the working class as a whole and the middle classes. In Figures 2.1 and 2.2 the extent of mobility between these two basic classes in four different time periods is shown, so that historical shifts can be

Figure 2.1   Working-class social mobility by marriage cohort, 1839–1914

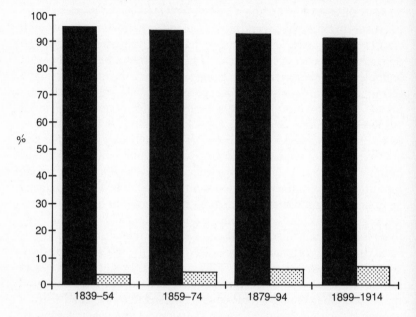

Key: ■ Percentage of men with working-class fathers remaining in the working class

⊞ Percentage of men with working-class fathers moving into the middle/upper class

identified. Two dimensions of mobility, both crucial to the process of demographic class formation, are illustrated here. On the one hand (Figure 2.1), we can see that only a very small proportion of all grooms whose fathers were working class had managed to achieve a middle-class 'destination' on marriage. The numbers increased over time, but even in 1914 somewhat fewer than one in ten workers' sons were crossing the major class barrier. From this perspective, the pre-First World War working class was clearly a very stable social collectivity. At the same time, if we alter the perspective, so that instead of considering the destinations of all those with working-class origins, we look back at the origins of all the grooms who ended up in the working class (Figure 2.2), the English working class also appears an extremely cohesive grouping. Throughout the period of analysis, nine out of every ten men

Figure 2.2   Working-class recruitment by marriage cohort, 1839–1914

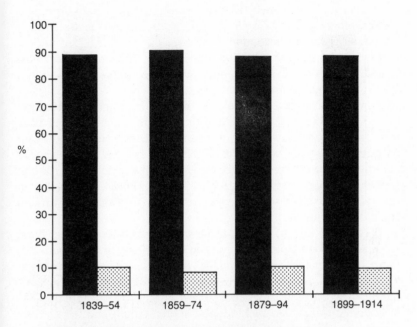

Key: ■ Percentage of working-class men with working-class fathers
⊞ Percentage of working-class men with middle/upper-class fathers

who were in a working-class occupation at the time of their marriage were themselves the sons of working-class men.

Prior to 1914 then, the English working class was a very stable and mature structural entity. Its members' horizons, whether they looked backwards or forwards, were severely restricted. Even those crossing into non-manual occupations rarely travelled far beyond the insecure margins of the middle class; most worked their way into a small business of some kind where the prospects of lasting success were poor, or alternatively they became clerks of some description, the majority enjoying pay and conditions not much better than the average skilled manual worker. It has always been recognised that a very sizeable proportion of small businessmen and white-collar employees hailed from working-class backgrounds (Lockwood 1958; Crossick 1978; Miles 1993b), but it must be understood that they were a very small minority of all those growing up in the shadow of the workshop, the factory, the mine or the 'big house'. Clerking might, as already noted, lead on to better things. A substantial number of bank clerks – up to half – could expect promotion to management (Savage 1993a). However, banking was one of the more prestigious occupations, and tended to recruit much less heavily from the working class than other white-collar sectors (Miles 1993c). In fact, the odds against someone from a working-class home becoming a member of the established middle class were monumental, starting at more than 200 to one against for skilled workers' sons, and extending by a factor of ten to more than 2,000 to one against among the unskilled.

However, this rather monolithic image is in important respects deceptive. Because there was relatively little movement into and away from the working class does not mean that there were not powerful barriers within the working class itself. In fact patterns of social mobility confirm that the axis of skill, which was vitally important in explaining income differentials, was also of central importance in separating the skilled working class from semi- and unskilled workers (Figures 2.3 and 2.4).

Taking just the first cohort, those who married between 1839 and 1854, whether we concentrate on the destinations of those with different working-class backgrounds, or the origins of those in different working-class positions, the figures are all high, and at the two poles of the class very substantial indeed. An astonishing four-fifths of the sons of skilled working-class men followed in their fathers' footsteps, while seven out of every ten men from the unskilled working class failed to move out of it. In terms of recruitment, over two-thirds of skilled workers came from skilled backgrounds, and over three-quarters of unskilled men were similarly 'self-recruited'. It follows that the rate of exchange between the top and bottom of the working class was extremely limited. Both the skilled and the unskilled sectors recruited just over 10 per cent of their membership from the other.

What is indicated here, therefore, is that the worlds of the skilled working class and the unskilled working class were largely isolated from each other, and this must obviously limit the extent to which we can talk about demographic working-class formation in this period. However, the crucial point is that the pattern did change over time, particularly for unskilled workers. Unskilled workers who married between 1899 and 1914 were much more likely to have come from skilled or semi-skilled backgrounds than was the case sixty years earlier, and by the same token the sons of unskilled men had greatly improved prospects of upward mobility inside the working class. On the eve of the First World War, half the unskilled manual workers still came from unskilled backgrounds, but the rate of recruitment from

Figure 2.3

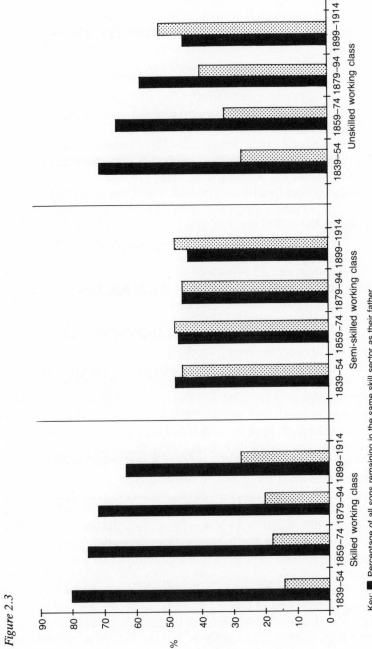

Key: ■ Percentage of all sons remaining in the same skill sector as their father
     ▨ Percentage of all sons moving elsewhere inside the working class

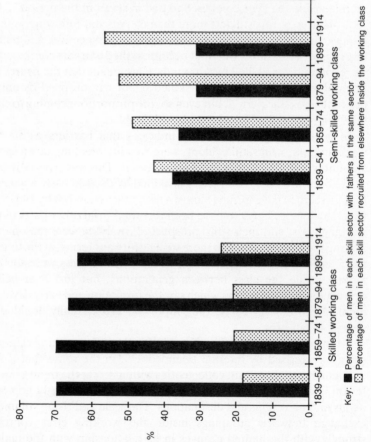

Figure 2.4

Key:
■ Percentage of men in each skill sector with fathers in the same sector
▨ Percentage of men in each skill sector recruited from elsewhere inside the working class

among the skilled had more than doubled, and altogether two out of every five unskilled workers had come from elsewhere inside the class. Similarly, while an unskilled future remained the fate of 44 per cent of men born at the bottom of society, a majority were now moving into skilled and semi-skilled positions.

A similar trend is evident among class IV, the semi-skilled working class. The proportion of semi-skilled workers whose fathers were in the same grouping fell less dramatically, from 38 per cent to 32 per cent, but by 1899–1914 over one-third came from skilled manual backgrounds, compared to less than a fifth sixty years earlier. At the same time the number of men born into semi-skilled families who made the step up to skilled status was also gradually increasing.

Skilled workers' sons, too, had become more mobile, although in rather less propitious ways. Almost a third were now downwardly mobile inside the class compared to one in seven in the period 1839–1854. However, this still left more than 60 per cent following in their fathers' footsteps, while, from the opposite perspective, a similarly large majority of those who had become skilled workers continued to be recruited from skilled backgrounds. This meant that the figures for internal recruitment within the skilled sector had dropped by only 5 per cent across the period, but even so, the proportions coming to class III from semi-skilled backgrounds still doubled.

In general, Figure 2.4 clearly indicates that barriers within the working class, while still evident, were steadily breaking down as the amount of mobility within the class increased. This was especially true at the bottom of the social scale: unskilled workers in early Victorian Britain seem to have formed almost a hereditary class, but by 1900 they were much more likely to have been recruited from other parts of the working class, and their sons' prospects of mobility were reasonable. Putting the overall picture in more straightforward terms, at the time of the Chartists only about one-fifth of the working class were socially mobile inside the class between generations, but just over half a century later, in the period which saw the formation and early development of the Labour Party, the proportion had virtually doubled to almost 40 per cent.

At the outbreak of the First World War, then, the working class was still characterised by internal boundedness, in the sense that it still contained very significant collectivities within it. Yet the trend towards fusion was strong. Members of this class were increasingly homogeneous in their origins and destinations. The scale and rising volume of exchange between groupings inside the working class contrasts strongly with the limited changes in its relationship with the middle classes. What we are clearly witnessing here, therefore, is the demographic 'making' of the English working class.

Unfortunately, Miles's analysis ends in 1914, but further evidence for later periods can be gained from the work of the twentieth-century sociologists Glass (1954) and Goldthorpe (1980 and 1987). Direct comparison with and between their data is not possible because they used different occupational classifications, but some general points can be made. First, it became more common for the sons of manual workers to move into the middle classes. The First World War seems to have had little effect on what was already a rising trend, although it is argued that educational reform helped to pave the way for more movement into the higher echelons of the middle class by skilled workers' sons, if not by any other sector of the working class (Waites 1987: 125). Glass's data suggest that in 1949 about 1 in 5 workers' sons with roughly comparable ages to those in Miles's study had moved into non-manual positions (Glass 1954: 186, Table 6). Goldthorpe's survey indicates a rather higher figure of 28 per cent for a comparable group, a figure which had risen to 36 per cent by 1972 (Goldthorpe 1980: Table 3.1). Interestingly, Goldthorpe's conclusion is that the increasing opportunities for working-class upward mobility in the twentieth century have resulted solely from the fact that, owing to the rapidly changing nature of the British economy, the number of middle-class jobs has outstripped the capacity of the middle class itself to fill them. In other words, he argues that the change in mobility patterns is not a reflection of a more 'open' society in which men from different social backgrounds have increasingly even chances of getting the same desirable job. By contrast, Miles suggests that the changes he has observed in the nineteenth and early twentieth centuries resulted from both a shift in the occupational structure and a clear trend towards greater openness (Miles 1993a). In other words, working-class homogenisation was driven by pressures (the universalisation of literacy, for example) making for greater equality of opportunity between men of skilled, semi-skilled and unskilled backgrounds, as well as the simple redistribution of personnel necessitated by the expansion of one sector at the expense of another.

The second main conclusion of the twentieth-century surveys is that mobility between the ranks of skilled and unskilled workers continued to increase. Glass's data show a rising tendency for movement from unskilled to skilled positions between generations, and Ginsberg's work on Bowley's post-war reappraisal of a pre-war survey of five industrial towns indicates the growing instability of the unskilled sector (Ginsberg 1929). Goldthorpe, in turn, found that as many unskilled workers came from skilled as unskilled manual backgrounds, while almost as many skilled workers' sons were downwardly mobile as managed to stay put (Goldthorpe 1980: Table 2.2). By the inter-war years, then, the axis of skill was of much reduced social significance within the working class, and although increasing numbers of manual workers' sons were moving into the middle class, the vast majority of manual workers came from working-class backgrounds. Confirming the pre-1914 pattern of separation between the classes, and the fundamental trend towards homogenisation within the working class, the extent of demographic class formation which these figures reveal is unquestionable.

The vast majority of research on social mobility concentrates on the experience of men. However, we have already indicated on pp. 23–5 that the experience of women in the labour market was different in important ways from that of men, and this was no less true of their mobility prospects. There is little available historical evidence of women's occupational mobility, but we have much more information about their patterns of marital mobility. Crossick (1978), Penn (1985), Miles (1992) and Mitch (1993) all show that nineteenth- and early twentieth-century women were more likely to move to a different social class by marrying a husband of a different social standing than were men who relied on moving into a different type of job. From the twentieth century, the similar picture revealed in Goldthorpe's work indicates that this is a long-term historical phenomenon (Goldthorpe 1987: 283, Table 10.2).

Prior to the First World War, the daughters of skilled working-class men married into the middle class at a rate of almost 10 per cent, compared to the 7 per cent of their 'brothers' who achieved a middle-class position via the labour market; similar disparities existed between the daughters and sons of semi- and unskilled workers (Miles 1992: 349, Table 6.1). This is obviously not a spectacular difference, but women also descended the social scale in larger proportions. Among the daughters of lower middle-class men, 57 per cent married into the working class. This compares unfavourably with the 47 per cent of lower middle-class sons finding jobs there, and whose chances of such downward mobility were also falling over time. Moreover, this particular disparity may well have grown over a lifetime, as the indications are that some of these men were only temporarily *déclassé*.

However, at the same time, the axis of skill was of less importance for women than for men. Although still divided by skill-based cultures, the internal polarities of the working class were never as strong for women as for men. As in the male labour market, though, the experience of working-class women in the marriage market was becoming much more homogeneous. The outcome of women's mobility experience was therefore somewhat paradoxical. The more effective forgers of intra-working class solidarities, and thus in one sense in the vanguard of demographic class formation, they were also more likely to undermine class stability and class cohesion by entering into class-crossing 'mixed' marriages.

CONCLUSIONS

A central point to have emerged from this discussion of demographic class formation is that the process is complicated and qualified by gender. We have shown that the male working class continued to be recruited almost exclusively from manual ranks, and that while class divisions for men were increasingly fixed and certain, the circumstances of women seem to have been rather more ambiguous. The barriers which divided middle class from working class were more frequently breached by women than by men, and as we have seen, women tended to be employed in jobs which were more likely to bring them into contact with the middle classes. Furthermore, for those considerable numbers of women who never married, the prospect of social mobility into the lower middle class was a real possibility. It was common for spinsters from working-class backgrounds to become schoolteachers or governesses, for instance, giving them a readier passage into the middle classes than their brothers (Hobsbawm 1964; Bradley 1989).

It is therefore understandable how, within the solidifying class system, questions of gender and the position of women produced a climate of moral panic among men. Because women defied such easy classification as men, and because they were more likely to transgress class boundaries, they might be perceived by men as a threat to the existing cultural order. The next chapter explores in greater detail the growing crisis of the skilled adult male in the labour market in order to show how such fears were related to structural developments in the economy.

3 Workplace independence and economic restructuring

Chapter 2 has shown that as boundaries between the skilled and unskilled lost their economic and social clarity, a more homogeneous working class emerged in the years after 1850. This descriptive exercise is, however, only a starting point. The fact that the working class became more homogeneous does not tell us how this process was interpreted by the people concerned or how it affected the potential for class-based collective action. Such growing uniformity could lead to greater sectionalism and division within the working class, as those skilled workers losing their privileges fought to defend them or saw their success or failure in individual terms. This chapter therefore explores how the restructuring of work and labour market relations affected relations between classes and within classes. We will show that the process of homogenisation discussed in Chapter 2 was indeed seen by skilled workers as a threat to the traditional autonomy of their work position, leading them to stage persistent defensive action. However, the second part of the chapter shows that the slow but unmistakable trend towards the bureaucratisation of the labour market which began from the late Victorian period ultimately served to politicise large sections of the working class, paving the way for a more militant and combative trade union movement.

MID-VICTORIAN CAPITALISM

There is a lingering image of nineteenth-century workers which presents them as hapless victims of a new, impersonal 'factory system' which both crushed their spirit and undermined their skills (for an early example, see Hammond and Hammond 1917). However, in recent years historians have shown that this view is misleading. Indeed, the wheel has swung full circle, with the current orthodoxy emphasising that the Victorian working class maintained a real independence from direct control in the workplace (Samuel 1977; Reid 1991). Mid-Victorian capitalism, it is argued, expanded not by crushing workers' skills, but by drawing on and utilising them.

Indeed, rather than employers being seen as a heroic social class, revolutionising their enterprises and sweeping all before them, recent literature suggests that they were actually rather marginal. Historians have argued that strategic control of the economy continued to lie in the hands of financiers, landlords and aristocrats. Lash and Urry (1987), drawing on the research of Lee (1979), have argued that Britain was a 'makler' economy which owed its dominant world position less to the mechanical superiority of its production techniques and more to its central trading role in the world economy (see also Ingham 1986). Cain and Hopkins (1986, 1993) have argued, in a similar vein, that Britain was characterised by a form of 'gentlemanly capitalism' in which industrialists were subservient to those who controlled finance and trade. One result was that industrialists were rarely able to breach the ranks of the upper-class elite. Rubinstein's (1981) research shows that for much of the nineteenth century the largest fortunes in Britain continued to be made not in industry, but in land and finance. Many of these fortunes were made in the south-east of England, where the economy expanded massively in the nineteenth century on the basis of its provision of services, not because of its industrial presence (Rubinstein 1987).

The view that industrialists were socially marginal has, in our view, been exaggerated (see Daunton 1989; Gunn 1988). The sources used by Rubinstein to assess wealth are biased strongly towards liquid forms of capital rather than the wealth tied up in fixed capital which is typical in business. It was not the fact that industrialists were economically and socially marginal which explains their reluctance to transform work relations, but rather the distinct business strategies they used (see generally Elbaum and Lazonick 1986; Harrison and Zeitlin 1985). In order to carry out their business employers relied very heavily on traditional, customary bonds which relied strongly on personal relationships and trust. Equally, products could most easily be sold if the manufacturer was reputable and could be trusted. Consequently industrialists had good reasons for cultivating the traditional social bonds which gave them standing in the business and local community.

The new breed of entrepreneurs therefore constituted a rather conservative group. Their main concern was to gain social recognition for their family dynasty and the 'family firm'. Many employers were less concerned with innovating in the production process than with establishing their 'name' by their social reputation. Employers therefore had good economic reasons for becoming respectable local worthies. They treated the new industrial town in a way not dissimilar to that in which squires had treated their country estates, as a dominion in which they might exercise moral, social and political leadership. Joyce (1980) and Garrard (1983) have discovered that employers frequently sought political careers, either in local government or as Members of Parliament for their towns. In some cases they actively aped the paternalism of the traditional landed classes by running country estates and building churches, schools, town halls or other civic amenities.

It is vital, however, to recognise the limits of this paternalism. It was largely a symbolic form of activity which rarely touched on matters of practical concern to workers, and had little impact on the methods of production or the day-to-day workings of the labour market. Joyce has shown that employers 'feted' their workers, and encouraged the communal celebration of dynastic events such as the marriage of a firm's family member. Rituals such as these played an important part in symbolising class boundaries and in cultivating among both employers and workers a proper sense of their respective positions. More direct involvement in the workers' lives was minimal, however. They seldom gave pensions or sick pay, were reluctant to take responsibility for employees injured in accidents, would usually lay off workers if business was slack, and would not usually promote employees to positions of authority in the firm. They reduced wage rates if trade was slow, regardless of the effect on their workforce. They very rarely provided housing for their employees, and when they did, it was used as a lever over workers who might be evicted if they left the firm or were troublesome.

This form of paternalism was therefore compatible with the existence of considerable amounts of worker autonomy. Employers relied upon labour-intensive methods of production based on workers' handicraft skills and talents, rather than substituting capital for labour through mechanisation. First recognised by the economic historian Clapham (1930) in the 1920s, this view has more recently been endorsed by Samuel (1977) and Musson (1978), and is now the orthodoxy. Steam power, for instance, was hardly used outside textiles, railways and mining as late as the 1870s. The typical British worker was employed in a workshop, among a small team of workers, using hand tools. Historians have been misled by focusing upon one industry – cotton textiles – where there had been technological advance, and one region – industrial Lancashire – where factories were well established (though even here they were often rather small – see

Farnie 1979). But in the Midlands major industrial expansion in the production of guns, jewellery, chains and ironware took place outside factories with workers frequently working at home or in small work-shops (Smith 1982). Similarly, mid-nineteenth-century Sheffield, home of the cutlery industry, saw production carried out in small enterprises by skilled craft workers (Pollard 1959).

It was not only that handicraft methods survived. Even in new industrial sectors, handicraft methods were adapted and found a new lease of life. Iron and steel shipbuilding, for instance, although concentrated in large shipyards on Clydeside, Tyneside and in Belfast, saw relatively little use of new technology or new working practices. Instead jobs were divided up into highly specialised areas among teams of skilled workers such as blacksmiths or platers. As a result management had little effective control over the process of production, the ships being built by teams of semi-independent skilled workers, each doing a particular task (McLelland and Reid 1985; Reid 1980).

Even in the most technologically advanced sectors of the economy, expansion after the early nineteenth century was based on the use of labour-intensive methods. In cotton textiles the main technological breakthroughs, the power loom and the self-acting mule, were in place from the 1840s, and were not significantly improved thereafter (Farnie 1979). After this date increases in productivity depended on workers being able to work harder and more efficiently on the same machines. The industry expanded as different towns specialised in certain types of cotton production. Preston became known for its fine quality cotton, Blackburn for its plain dhooties, Burnley for medium-weight grey cloths and so on. The result was that employees' skills became more and more refined and employers relied on them more as the century wore on (Savage 1988a).

This was reflected in changing patterns of work training. In the traditional model, which had been in decline since the eighteenth century and was formally abolished in 1814 (Rule 1986), a 14-year-old worker would be indentured to a master who would ensure that he would be taught the skills (or 'mystery') of the trade. At the age of 21 the apprentice would become a journeyman, a fully accredited skilled worker. By the late nineteenth century, More (1980) argues that very few trades indeed were able to regulate and control their labour market. The Webbs showed that in the 1890s only 600,000 workers, no more than 3–4 per cent of the workforce, could enforce restrictions on entry to the trade through apprenticeship controls (Webb and Webb 1902: 474). However, a diffuse cultural ethos of apprenticeship re-mained important. In some cases workers were still formally indentured to employers, while in others they learnt by 'picking up' skills from fellow workers. This might involve the informal learning of tasks from workmates but, especially in capital-intensive industries such as the railways, iron or steel, it meant climbing a job ladder in which the performance of one job also allowed workers to pick up the skills of the next. Although workers enjoyed considerable autonomy in the workplace, it would be mistaken to exaggerate the degree of trade union control over the labour market.

The predominance of this form of skill acquisition explains the high degree of occupational continuity which is often found within families, as fathers would frequently train their sons in the skills of their job. Miles's (1992) analysis of social mobility provides the remarkable statistic that no less than 44 per cent of sons were in an occupation identical to their fathers' in the mid-nineteenth century.

The important feature of this form of training is that it allowed workers considerable freedom and leverage since employers played little part in it. It was also common for skilled workers to recruit their own assistants, and in many cases an 'internal contractor' would take responsibility for the recruitment and control of work groups (Littler 1982). Even in the bureaucratic railway companies gangers would be employed to check that the track was in good condition on a given stretch of rail, and it was the ganger's responsibility to organise any necessary repairs. It was also common for men to employ their own wives and children to work under them (Mark-Lawson and Witz 1988); in such cases the men would be paid a lump sum which they would be responsible for handing on. In many larger works foremen and over-lookers often had a great deal of discretion over hiring, firing and discipline, and these supervisory workers would frequently employ their own family members, friends or contacts (Melling 1980). In the cotton-weaving industry overlookers would employ their wives and children, as well as neighbourhood contacts (Savage 1985).

In general, employers delegated responsibility, allowing skilled male workers to carve out a role as key agents in the direction and recruitment of labour. Some writers have argued that after 1850 a group of labour aristocrats who controlled other workers emerged, with a vested interest in exploiting those beneath them (Hobsbawm 1964; Foster 1974; Gray 1981; Breuilly 1992). But, while drawing attention to important divisions within the working class, the idea of a distinct labour aristocracy is unhelpful. The practice of informal work control and pride in a trade were taken up by very large numbers of manual workers and were not confined to a small worker elite. Even where a distinct supervisory or elite grade could be distinguished, its members were agents of a wider set of craft values which were more widely shared within the working class (McClelland 1987); if they defied wider working-class values they might be subject to criticism. It is notable that when an overlooker was accused of sexual harassment against female weavers in north-east Lancashire there was a widespread outcry and sanctions against the man were imposed (Lambertz 1985). It was also quite common for foremen to belong to trade unions (Melling 1980).

These handicraft skills had ambiguous implications. While workers may have gained by being able to enjoy a degree of autonomy and control at work, the price they paid was reliance on insecure market conditions. Stinchcombe (1959) has pointed out that employers frequently prefer to use labour-intensive methods of production when their business is insecure due to fluctuations in the trade cycle. Rather than invest valuable money in machinery or premises, employers simply take on more workers when business is good and dispense with them when business is bad. In this way their money will not be tied up in machinery which lies idle.

For these reasons, lack of security was the price workers paid for their independence. This explains why workers were so concerned to guard against the effects of unemployment or bad health by mutual support and protection. Workers realised that their employers had no great loyalty to them and would dispense with their labour when it suited them. Workers had to look after their own interests since no one else would. This understanding focused working-class energies on finding ways of coping with the immediate contingencies of everyday life; being able to look after oneself and one's family in good times and bad was the ultimate guarantee of respectability. This led to the construction of an elaborate network of worker-controlled mutual provision, in the form of friendly societies, trade unions, medical clubs and the like.

These types of working relations also helped to construct vital distinctions between the respectable and unrespectable working class. Households were respectable if they could provide for themselves without recourse to charity or the state (Roberts 1984). Respectability meant independence, the ability to stand on your own two feet, its most emotive instance being the attempt to put money by to cover funeral expenses, avoiding the humiliation of a pauper's grave. While most workers attempted to be respectable, many lacked the economic resources to escape the brutal realities of low pay and poverty. Some workers had to give up trying to plan for the future, and simply attempted to survive by any means possible, whether this meant petty criminality, charity or – the last resort – the workhouse. This incapacity was particularly common in large cities and conurbations. Here the nineteenth century saw the development of a casual labour market where large numbers of workers found it difficult to find permanent work and tried to eke out a living in whatever way they could (Treble 1979; Stedman Jones 1971). Benson (1989) estimates that as many as 10 per cent became street traders in the attempt to make ends meet. Even those who did manage to find paid employment had no security. In the docks, workers were employed by the hour (Stedman Jones 1971; Phillips and Whiteside 1985). The problem was not entirely an urban one: in the countryside agricultural labourers found it difficult to earn enough to meet their basic needs, although some had allotments or gardens in which they could grow some of their own food.

The important feature of this type of distribution of poverty is that skilled workers could regard themselves as aloof from it. They frequently lost their jobs, but they prided themselves on the range of protective institutions which gave them a degree of security, and they could usually rely on procuring a job when trade picked up. It also remained common for unemployed skilled workers to move round the country looking for work (Southall 1991). Most skilled workers were therefore able to avoid falling into the ranks of the unskilled. Even in London, which suffered a particularly intense decline in skilled manual work after 1850, only around 20 per cent of those moving into dock work, a particularly insecure and marginal form of employment, had previously been skilled workers. As Stedman Jones (1984: 75) notes, those skilled workers who did end up in labouring jobs probably had reputations as drunkards or trouble makers.

In general skilled workers did not sympathise with the plight of the poor or the casually employed, because to do so would undermine the very moral foundations on which their position lay (McClelland 1987). The possession of a 'trade', which they even regarded as their 'property' (Rule 1986), placed them in a different position from the predominantly unskilled who were forced to rely on the casual labour market, and it severely limited the extent to which cultural bridges between the skilled and unskilled could be crossed.

As well as helping to produce a chronic horizontal split within the working class, the independence of labour also led to endemic sectionalism among skilled workers themselves (see Reid 1980; Penn 1985). Workers always had to be on guard against other groups of workers who might seek to claim a particular job as theirs. Demarcation disputes between workers were frequent especially in situations where new jobs were emerging, and conflict with employers was frequently deflected into conflicts among workers. Sectionalism also took a highly localised form, as workers in various neighbourhoods and towns were suspicious of collaborating with others. One of the main stumbling blocks of early trade unionism was the reluctance of many union branches to pay funds to a central headquarters because they feared that these monies might be misappropriated (e.g. Bagwell 1963 on railway trade unionism).

The mid-Victorian labour market reinforced divisions within the working class by turning labour inwards. Responsible for recruitment, training and supervision, workers would police their own labour markets; this led to endemic conflicts between different groups of skilled workers while also making those without access to a skill responsible for their own fate.

THE DEVELOPMENT OF IMPERSONAL CAPITALISM, 1880–1950

The years after 1880 saw a series of slow but distinct changes which altered the relations discussed above. The most important developments were the rise of impersonal capitalism with the bureaucratic forms of labour management and labour market organisation associated with them. The rise of the large business corporation in place of the small family firm was particularly important here. Following parliamentary legislation on 'limited liability' in the mid-Victorian period, it became possible for firms to sell shares, so allowing ownership of firms to fragment. People could buy shares, knowing that if the firm went bankrupt they were liable to lose only the value of their shares, not all their assets as had been the case previously. The average size of firms began to increase rapidly as many small firms merged together in order to deal with competition. This process continued for much of the early twentieth century, so that by 1930 the 100 largest firms accounted for 26 per cent of the total manufacturing output, a figure very similar to that in the USA where the rise of the large corporation was well known (Hannah 1976, Appendix 2). By the 1930s many large corporations – Courtaulds, Shell, ICI, Unilever, Boots, W.H. Smith and so on – had reached a prominent position in the British economy.

However, although the large firm seemed to have become dominant by the inter-war years a number of qualifications have to be made. These large companies were often organised as 'holding companies'. This meant that the corporation structure was simply a legal shell under which smaller companies operated with a large amount of *de facto* autonomy. Consequently firms did not operate as an integrated whole, and might continue traditional ways of working and managing. Indeed, some of these large corporations were not so much a new form of economic organisation as a means of managing decline. Especially in the years after 1918 the government encouraged rationalisation of firms in order to reduce excess capacity. An example was the Lancashire Cotton Corporation, which was formed with the express intention of shutting down redundant plant and machinery. These large companies were as much a hangover of old industrial forms as the dynamos of a new modern economy.

Old dynastic interests could also use a corporate shell to defend their position. Scott (1988) has charted how many leading families have successfully retained effective power in firms, even when their shareholdings form only a tiny fraction of the total. In Britain family members continued to have decisive control in the reconstituted companies, whereas in the USA effective power was vested in managers. Many of the most successful British companies such as Cadbury, Rowntree, Pilkington, Boots, Courtaulds and the like indicate by their name the extent to which they continued to be family-controlled. As a result, Chandler (1990) argues that Britain has not experienced the full development of modern corporate firms, as the USA has, but instead has seen a hybrid form of 'personal capitalism' in which older family influence is perpetuated and the development of a professional management cadre is retarded (see also Savage *et al.* 1992).

These are indications that the rise of the large firm did not mark a revolutionary change in production relations. Employers, increasingly subject to foreign competition, still sought to reduce their production costs by relying on labour-intensive methods. Whereas in the USA some employers, such as Henry Ford, were prepared to boost wages in return for productivity increases made possible by capital investment in plant and machinery, in Britain employers were rarely prepared to countenance paying anything more than the minimum they could get away with. Many of the most striking innovations brought in by employers – such as the premium bonus system in engineering (Burgess 1985, Price 1985, 1986) – were concerned simply to devise payment systems by which lower wages could be paid for a given amount of work. There was little systematic attempt to deskill. Lazonick (1983) has explored how cotton employers met foreign competition by switching to cheaper, poor-quality raw cotton, putting even greater emphasis upon the skills of the cotton operatives to produce good-quality cloth out if it. Even where new technology was introduced, for instance the linotype machine which became common in printing from the 1890s, printing workers were able to re-establish craft control of the production process (Zeitlin 1979).

Only a few firms adopted 'scientific management' (see Braverman 1974) which broke up craft groups, leading to the sub-division of work tasks, time and motion studies, and more piecework (Littler 1982). Scientific management envisaged a much more active role for managers in allocating and supervising work than was found under the old craft system. Although a number of firms experimented with such techniques (Littler 1982), on the whole craft autonomy prevailed (Cronin 1984). Zeitlin (1980) has even argued that in new areas such as motor car manufacture, handicraft methods of production and old forms of craft control were re-established.

There were some significant changes. Glucksmann (1990) has shown that assembly line methods were used in the new industries of the inter-war years. Firms such as Peek Frean (biscuits), Morphy Richards (radios), EMI (gramophones), Hoover (vacuum cleaners) and Lyons (food processing) developed systems where unskilled women workers would be employed to carry out routine tasks on a moving conveyor belt. However, it is important not to lose a sense of perspective. Assembly line production actually involved only 1 or 2 per cent of the workforce. Many sectors of the new industry continued to use old-fashioned sweated labour. Radio manufacturers and cabinet makers in Slough, for example, employed young boys, girls and women on exceptionally low piece-rate wages to carry out simple assembly jobs (Savage 1988b). Furthermore, many firms involved in new forms of production continued to be small and unstable (Foreman-Peck 1985).

Glucksmann does, however, point to a vital change: the declining importance of adult male workers. As employers sought to reduce their labour costs, they turned in many cases to female and youth labour, which allowed them to pay lower wages. Bradley (1989) has shown that the 1880s and 1890s saw a considerable increase in the use of young female labour in pottery, shoemaking and hosiery. In the textile industry, where they were already working in large numbers, the proportion of women employed in weaving continued to increase steadily. Women were also introduced into many types of traditionally male employment during the First World War (Braybon 1980), and although they were removed from many of these sectors shortly afterwards, there were some areas, notably clerical work, in which they were retained in large numbers. Women were also used in very large numbers in the 'new industries' which developed between the wars. The female workforce rose by 650,000 between 1921 and 1938

(Glucksmann 1990: 40). The employment of younger women rose especially rapidly.

This growth of female labour caused a certain tension for skilled men, whose patriarchal authority might thus be laid open to challenge. Equally threatening in some sectors was the growing use of boy labour. In the engineering industry especially employers would attempt to abuse the apprenticeship system by taking on boy apprentices on low wages but then dismissing them when they were qualified. The extended use of youth labour was also well established in large bureaucratic environments such as the railways and the Post Office. Childs (1987) argues that the substitution of adult male by boy labour was evident in boot and shoe manufacture, printing, cabinet making, cutlery and docking. In 1911, 71 per cent of messengers, 30 per cent of cotton workers, 28 per cent of woollen workers and 23 per cent of pottery and glass workers were boys under the age of 20.

The position of adult men was further weakened after 1918. Many of the staple traditional industries were exposed to fierce competition from overseas. Those very industries where the skilled independent male worker had been concentrated were worst affected by the trade depressions of the 1920s and the major slump which began in 1930. For example, 41 per cent of coal miners were unemployed in 1932, 31 per cent of cotton workers – although here women were more likely to be made unemployed than men (Savage 1988a) – 60 per cent of ship-builders, and 49 per cent of iron and steel workers. In 1932, the total unemployed reached 2,745,000, around 23 per cent of the manual labour force, while in Wales, the worst-hit area, over one-third of the workforce was unemployed.

The development of mass unemployment had major repercussions on divisions within the working class. The typical image of the unemployed was male – pictures of desolate men hanging around street corners or searching for work are legion (see e.g. Stevenson and Cook 1979). Even though female unemployment was a considerable problem it was not treated with much seriousness by government or social commentators. But the rise of mass unemployment served to bridge the rift between male skilled and unskilled wommrkers which had existed in Victorian times. The slump was not just a cyclical recession in which skilled men could expect to find work when trade picked up. It marked a permanent downturn in the fortunes of traditional industries and therefore the redundancy of the skills on which they had depended. Both skilled and unskilled workers lost their jobs, and such was the extent of unemployment in many industrial areas that there was little chance of even skilled men finding work. Whereas in the Victorian period poverty had tended to drive a wedge between skilled and unskilled, by the inter-war years it helped to unite them in the face of a common problem.

The position of skilled men was further threatened by increased bureaucratic control in the labour market, eroding their autonomy in recruitment and training. In the cotton industry, for instance, decisions about hiring and firing were taken out of the hands of overlookers and reserved for the shed managers. Melling (1980, 1983) has shown how firms attempted to remove their supervisors from the social and cultural world of the workers by emphasising their special status and privileges, encouraging them to identify with the firm. As we have already seen in Chapter 2, the wages of foremen and supervisors rose considerably relative to other workers. Firms demanded that their supervisory workers renounce union membership, and encouraged them to join societies specifically created for them, such as the Foremen's Mutual Benefit Society in shipbuilding. Some firms introduced company housing schemes in which foremen and supervisors were given superior-quality premises in order to emphasise their detachment from other workers, while pension rights and machinery for collective representation also emphasised the special status of these workers (Melling 1983). On the railways many supervisory workers, such as station masters and goods inspectors, had been sympathetic to trade unions, and some even joined the 1911 and 1919 strikes. In 1919, 24 per cent of supervisory grades on the Great Western struck alongside their subordinates. But by the time of the 1926 General Strike very few supervisors were prepared to defy the companies by striking (Savage 1993b).

In 1880 the state had virtually no role in the labour market, except insofar as the Poor Law provided minimal provision for those who were destitute, often by forcing them to move into workhouses where they effectively gave up their freedom in return for subsistence. The increase in state intervention thereafter had a major impact. In 1908 Labour Exchanges were created in all major urban areas, providing an institutional centre in which workers could register as unemployed and employers could advertise vacancies. Many unions were fiercely hostile to these Labour Exchanges which they saw as undercutting their own role in controlling labour markets. The Labour Exchanges were not widely used by employers to seek workers except in special circumstances such as the labour shortages of the First World War, but they did become important as sites where workers 'signed on' to claim benefit. Vincent (1993) has also shown that schools played a more important role in placing young workers in jobs, with increasing numbers of employers paying attention to school references and recruiting through examination. Juvenile Employment Bureaux helped guide young workers into 'appropriate jobs'.

The development of a national insurance system took the bureaucratisation of the labour market a step further. This scheme, introduced for some workers in 1911 and extended to most industrial workers in 1920, meant that workers, employers and the state each paid contributions to a fund which would be used to grant sickness and unemployment benefit. National insurance benefits were framed in such a way that they paid enough to keep a worker in reasonable fitness. In the inter-war years benefits were reasonably generous, especially where local authorities gave in to pressure from the Labour movement.

The state also intervened in other ways. At the local level it became increasingly active from the end of the nineteenth century, providing municipal amenities such as gas, water and electricity (Thane 1991). Most councils also agreed to pay wages at trade union rates to prevent 'good' employers being undercut. At times this went much further and in the 1890s extensive intervention was claimed to be a form of municipal socialism, for instance in east London and Glasgow (Buck 1981; Smyth 1991). Many municipal employees – paviours, refuse collectors and so forth – had come from among the most casualised ranks of unskilled labour, and local authority action could therefore significantly improve their position. Indeed, in some cases the state intervened directly to decasualise labour, for example on the docks (Phillips and Whiteside 1985).

Bureaucratic employers took greater steps to monitor and control the progress of their workers. The railways had always exercised strong punitive discipline (Kingsford 1970; McKenna 1980), with workers being fined, dismissed or demoted for negligence or breaching regulations. From the 1880s even greater surveillance of workers took place, with regular medical tests and examinations of competence (Price 1985, 1986). A worker who started at the age of 14 wishing to become an engine driver had his competence to drive investigated no fewer than three times by specialist examiners who would assess whether he could fire the engine, drive safely, and recite the company rules and regulations. His health record become the subject of increasing scrutiny, with annual sight tests introduced from the turn of the century (Savage 1993b).

These developments meant that the informal labour market, policed by skilled male workers, was threatened by the emergence of an increasingly formalised and bureaucratised one. When someone began work he or she would have to deal with a manager or foreman to whom national insurance cards had to be submitted. These documents would usually be stored in the works office. Thus the organisation of the labour market was taken away from the workers and placed in the hand of managers and officials.

It is possible to exaggerate the degree of change. In some sectors of the economy workers continued to find work in much the same informal way as they had always done. The old 'extended internal labour market' where family members would help find work for their relatives persisted even beyond 1945. Yet the trend towards the break-up of recruitment of this sort is clear, even if it was incomplete. Miles's (1992) analysis of social mobility shows that only 31 per cent of men marrying between 1899 and 1914 worked in the same occupation as their fathers, compared to 47 per cent in the period 1859–74. His analysis of working-class autobiographies also indicates that the major shift in methods of finding work between the eighteenth and the early twentieth centuries was 'away from the informal mechanism, and towards the more structured and meritocratic modes of engagement' (Miles 1993a: 33; see also Vincent 1993). One of the few contemporary surveys tracing the way that young people found work showed that by the mid-1930s only 34 per cent of boys and 28 per cent of girls found work in the traditional way through the influence of family friends (Jewkes and Jewkes 1938: 34).

These developments both posed a threat and offered an opportunity for skilled male labour. They put traditional modes of recruitment and labour discipline into question, and so threatened the traditional authority of the skilled men. Yet they also offered these same workers greater resources and opportunities should they be able to influence the bureaucratic mechanisms to their advantage. State intervention politicised workers who had to mobilise to prevent their previously informal influence being undermined as well as to agitate for other forms of state intervention which might help them.

Unionisation was therefore, in many cases, an attempt to find a formal voice for workers in a new context in which informal modes of communication and co-ordination were losing their currency. Trade unions had a long history, growing out of strong preindustrial craft traditions (Rule 1986). Union traditions were forced to go under-ground in the early nineteenth century when they were banned under the Combination Acts, but they re-emerged in the 1830s and 1840s after these Acts were repealed, and for short periods of time the new 'general unions' attracted large memberships. It was only in the years after 1850, however, that some smaller unions developed a strong institutional and therefore long-lasting presence, but for most of the Victorian period only a minority of the best-paid and most skilled workers belonged – perhaps around 10 per cent of the workforce. By the later 1880s this situation had changed dramatically. Following the London dockers' strike in 1889, unionisation increased considerably among previously ununionised workers, mainly unskilled but including some from established trades. Membership fluctuated enormously, rising and falling in the early 1890s, and then rising from only 2 million in 1910 to reach over 8 million in 1920, at which point nearly half the workforce was unionised. This level could not be sustained in the Depression and membership fell to just over 4 million by 1933 before rising again slightly (Cronin 1984).

Some employers were actually keen to encourage trade union growth, as part of a new bureaucratic machinery. In the cotton industry, the first industry where unionisation spread beyond craft workers to embrace the semi-skilled and unskilled (Turner 1962), employers recognised that strong trade unions which could enforce 'list prices' would make it difficult for small, marginal firms to set up and attempt to survive by paying low wages which undercut the larger companies. Employers were also content to recognise the development of unions in engineering (Zeitlin 1985).

In other cases unionisation was related to the bureaucratisation of firms. Railway trade unionism was encouraged by the waning patience of railway companies with informal deputations of workers. Traditionally railway workers had sent in petitions, or 'memorials', followed by a deputation to the Board of Directors whenever they had a grievance (Bagwell 1963). In 1880 the chairman of the Great Western Railway Company, Sir Daniel Gooch, responded to a petition from footplate workers for a reconsideration of pay and working conditions not by considering the merits of the petition, but by saying to the deputation, 'Damn the signatures, have you got the men?' His direct incitement to the deputation to see if they had the muscle to bring out the drivers on strike led to the GWR becoming one of the strongest bases of the footplate workers union, ASLEF.

The rise of state intervention was both a response to unionisation and an encouragement to further union growth. It is no accident that union membership increased dramatically during the First World War when the state took over the co-ordination and management of large parts of industry and the labour market. The experience of the First World War made workers aware of the potential of unions as a force which might act as a lever on the state to protect or improve their conditions (Reid 1985). In some cases unions continued to be deeply hostile to state activity, as in the cotton industry where they continued to campaign for the end of national insurance legislation. But given the scale of state intervention, unions had little option but to accept it.

CONCLUSIONS

The rise of unionism can be understood as a defensive reaction to changed labour market conditions, an attempt to restore by formal, institutional action the autonomy and discretion of skilled men which was under threat. Yet it was a highly complex process. While in some ways a reaction to the more formal labour market, unionisation itself provided a further impetus towards bureaucratisation. It had both defensive and progressive elements, as workers experimented with new ways of reconstituting lost authority, through workers' control or state control (Holton 1976). And, while owing a great deal to the struggles of privileged skilled workers, unionisation spread well beyond this sector. With the development of New Unionism from the late 1880s general unions began to recruit semi- and unskilled workers (Price 1985; Cronin 1979; Hobsbawm 1985). In some cases the union- isation of skilled men provided an incentive for semi- and unskilled workers to unionise in order to defend their particular interests. In others it was a reaction to the continued drive by employers to reduce labour costs.

Two points are of particular importance for the argument of this book. First, these events testify to the declining salience of the distinction between skilled and unskilled which we discussed in Chap- ter 2. As we have shown, in the mid-Victorian period there was a major distinction between those labour markets in which skilled workers could police their own work and those where casual labour meant the breakdown of any sort of regulation. By the inter-war years the development of more bureaucratic procedures meant that all workers had to work in a similar labour market. Second, the state's role in the labour market served to politicise labour issues in a new way. They were now matters for public concern. State intervention allowed the public (and private) dissemination of knowledge about levels of unem- ployment, wage rates and strikes. It also meant that conflicts between capital and labour, or between groups of labourers, could not be carried out in a private realm, but only in a public arena. For this reason, it became increasingly difficult for conflicts to be confined to the industrial level alone. The state was a legitimate terrain for class conflict.

4 Working-class formation and the city

Class formation is a spatial process. Cities, towns, villages and rural areas come to bear social meanings which associate them with particular social groups. People build forms of organisation and identity on territorial bases, and these sites may affect the forms of collective action open to them. Where individuals are spread over wide areas, so that they rarely have contact with others in a similar position to themselves, it will probably be much more difficult for them to form the bonds and social ties which would help them to participate in social action than it is for people who live alongside neighbours who are in the same boat.

This chapter explores the spatial formation of the working class in the British city. In Victorian times, industrial cities were home to a nascent middle-class elite, which left its indelible stamp on the physical form and social organisation of the city. So long as this was the case, it proved difficult for the working class to develop a distinct urban presence. However, in the course of the late nineteenth and early twentieth centuries, the elite tended to distance itself from urban life, and industrial cities were increasingly defined as working-class spaces. It was from this territorial axis that working-class formation occurred.

MIDDLE-CLASS HEGEMONY IN THE VICTORIAN INDUSTRIAL CITY

Cities were not the automatic product of industrialisation. London, in particular, was well established, with 500,000 inhabitants in 1701 and nearly a million a century later (Garside 1990). There were other old-established medieval cities such as Norwich and Bristol. But contemporaries were in no doubt that the development of trade and industry brought the growth of new towns and cities which had hardly existed in 1700. Manchester, Leeds, Liverpool, Birmingham and Sheffield all grew from obscure origins to become cities with over 100,000 people by the early nineteenth century and appeared to be harbingers of a new type of commercial city. These large cities emerged as provincial capitals of new industrial areas, specialising not only in manufacturing but also in trade and commerce. In their wake, a large number of smaller, but still populous towns developed, and it was often in those, for example Oldham, Blackburn, Wolverhampton and Wakefield, that industry was most concentrated. In 1750 there were only six towns or cities with more than 20,000 inhabitants and only 13.7 per cent of people lived in them (and most of these lived in London): by 1801 there were sixteen such towns with 18.6 per cent of the population. By 1851, 37.6 per cent of people lived in such towns, by 1881 a majority, 52.9 per cent of the population (Corfield 1982; Waller 1983).

These new towns and cities seemed to mark a break from an older urban milieu. Nineteenth-century social commentators frequently saw them as the home of a newly created working class. Frederick Engels's famous study of Manchester and Salford, *The Condition of the Working Class in England in 1844*, regarded the city as manifesting new forms of poverty and inequality. He pointed to very high degrees of residential segregation between the working classes, crammed together in the worst housing, sometimes living in cellars, and the rich middle classes. He argued that the city produced a new form of social indifference in which the middle and upper classes abandoned any sense of responsibility for the poor, and he predicted that Manchester would become the centre of a working-class revolt as a result.

Yet, in fact, Engels's account ignores the fact that the working class, far from being out of the sight and mind of the urban middle classes, was in fact the subject of constant observation and surveillance. Social observers, from public health officials trying to map out areas of disease, to those such as Henry Mayhew and Charles Booth who carried out more detached research, attempted to examine the social geography of the new urban spaces precisely in order to locate and inspect the working class, and make them visible to the middle classes. In the best-known slum areas such as the East End of London, many institutions, from the Charity Organisation Society to religious missions and settlement houses, attempted to introduce middle-class influence (Stedman Jones 1971).

What was striking about these new towns and cities was the extent to which the middle classes claimed the right to survey – in the name of health, education and morality – vast swathes of working-class residence. The new towns were vital constituents of middle-class identity, and any potential threat was watched with suspicion and concern.

Borsay (1989) has shown that as early as the eighteenth century an 'urban renaissance' allowed a new middle class of traders, manufacturers, professional interests and merchants to develop a range of modern urban civic amenities in new provincial cities, such as Preston, Warwick, Shrewsbury and Leominster. Even though urbanisation leapt into a new dimension after 1800, as the proportion of the population living in cities of over 100,000 people grew from 11 per cent in 1801 to 44 per cent by 1901, the middle classes continued to rely on the towns and cities as the places in which their authority rested. They continued to play a key role in defining and controlling the new urban fabric.

It has long been thought that one of the major contrasts between the preindustrial city and the industrial city is that the wealthy and powerful tended to live at the centre of the former, but away from the centre in the latter, leaving central urban districts to be colonised by businesses and the working class (Sjoberg 1960; Dennis 1984). Recent research has shown, however, that in many industrial cities the middle classes continued to live in the central locations well into the nineteenth century. In Preston, for instance, the main elite residential area around Winckley Square was only a minute's walk from the central shopping streets, and similar patterns were found elsewhere, for instance in Huddersfield (Dennis 1984: Figure 7.5). David Ward's (1975) study of Leeds argues that segregation actually seemed to be declining between 1851 and 1871, and only the extremely wealthy had clearly separated off to live apart. Elsewhere labourers, skilled workers, traders and the lower middle classes tended to live in the same areas, undermining Engels's claims that new homogeneous working-class areas were in evidence by this time (see Dennis 1984).

The extent of middle-class involvement in the early industrial city has been examined in detail by R.J. Morris (1983, 1990). Morris has shown that the city was vital to the identity of the new middle classes, who defined themselves in opposition to the landed aristocracy and the London establishment. As towns grew and gained legal powers of self-government (the 1835 Municipal Corporation Act being an important landmark) middle-class notables engaged in efforts to gain cultural legitimacy for their towns. One element of this was the grand Gothic architecture which characterised the Victorian city. In some cases, such as the Free Trade Hall in Manchester, built to celebrate the repeal of the Corn Laws in 1846, the building was named as a direct testament to the political success of the middle classes over the aristocracy. In other cases, the middle classes helped to fund the construction of a grand cityscape of churches, libraries and town halls. Gothic architecture – harking back to medieval building styles – helped to give historical roots to the new towns. The same point was also reinforced by the commissioning of local histories, and the building of local museums and art galleries. In this way the historical legitimacy of the middle classes could be established.

The new towns and cities saw the elaboration of a public realm of parks, libraries and roads where spectacles of urban grandeur could be constructed and appreciated. Yet these public spaces were in reality colonised by the middle classes. Morris (1990) has given especial attention to the role of the voluntary associations in the provincial capitals, such as Leeds. These associations, such as literary and philosophical societies, mechanics institutes, and local charities, played a crucial role in local cultural life and helped to establish urban identity. Morris argues that since the middle classes were frequently divided – by religion, politics or occupation – these institutions allowed a forum in which an otherwise disparate class could unite. Furthermore, it was the middle classes who effectively held the reins of urban power. Given the fact that (until 1882) councillors needed to be significant property owners and were also required to attend day-time meetings, the vast majority of the working urban population were precluded from standing for election until the very end of the Victorian period (Garrard 1983; Hennock 1973).

This is not to say that there was a single middle-class elite which governed all the cities as if they were personal fiefs. The middle classes were divided by party politics (between Liberal and Tory) and religion (Dissenters against Anglicans), as well as occupation and background, and the Victorian period saw endemic conflict between various parties. The broader 'civic project' of establishing the social, cultural and political legitimacy of the city fell overwhelmingly on large manufacturers and industrialists. Hennock (1973) has shown how much Victorian urban politics was organised around a conflict between small business people, concerned to keep the rates down in order to improve their own economic position, and the large industrialists, who were more prepared to countenance public spending in order to improve the standing of 'their' city. In most industrial towns manufacturers formed the largest single group of councillors (Garrard 1983; Joyce 1980).

The Victorian city was therefore a space which announced and celebrated the arrival of the middle class. Yet there was a major problem for the new urban middle class: they were in the numerical minority in those very cities which they used to establish their identity. The vast majority of urban dwellers were working class. The resulting insecurity led to middle-class attempts to colonise working-class areas, to try to reinforce middle-class hegemony.

These cities were cosmopolitan, not conducive to the creation of fixed community sentiments which are produced by long-term population stability. Cities were still growing fast, fuelled by migration from the countryside. Such was the impact of migration that in 1851 less than half the population of many cities had actually been born in them (Dennis 1984: Table 2.3), and if the calculations exclude children, who are most likely to have been born in the city, it is possible that around three-quarters of adults were migrants. Many skilled workers continued the practice of 'tramping', of moving to a different location in order to seek work, and Southall (1991) shows that in years of severe depression, such as 1842/43, one-quarter of the members of one trade society moved location. Most urban migrants moved short distances, often from a rural hinterland to the nearest large town (Anderson 1971). Southall has shown that in 1851 skilled workers in their thirties lived, on average, under 20 miles from their place of birth, suggesting that mobility was short range. Many town dwellers continued to have strong ties to the countryside around them.

People regularly moved house in the Victorian city. In the mid-nineteenth century around a quarter of the population moved each year, with only around a third living at one address for five years (Dennis 1984: Table 8.1). Admittedly many people moved only short distances, and might still have frequented the same local shops and public houses. Nonetheless, the development of social networks where people could rely on neighbours for help and support cannot have been aided by high residential turnover, although there were some neighbourhoods which did develop strong solidarities. In Sheffield, for instance, skilled workers in the cutlery industry became notorious in the 1860s for intimidating their neighbours into observing craft customs (Smith 1982). Yet Sheffield was somewhat exceptional, with two-thirds of its 1851 population being locally born (Dennis 1984: Table 2.3). Its strong attachment to neighbourhood organisation was also manifested in demands for neighbourhood assemblies in the Chartist years of the 1840s (Smith 1982).

More usually, working-class neighbourhoods were subject to surveillance from the middle classes. Joyce (1980) has shown how, in Lancashire, employers carved out their influence in neighbourhood life, to the extent that workers tended to vote in accord with the politics of the local millowner. In some cases there were complete 'factory colonies', as in Saltaire near Leeds where Titus Salt built houses and amenities for his workers (Reynolds 1983; Jowitt 1986). More commonly, leading employers would help to finance local churches and schools in different parts of the city, and would often play leading roles in directing and controlling them. These would help to organise social life and provide a cultural focus in the area which would, in turn, tend to forestall working-class organisation and activity.

The result was to disorganise many urban neighbourhoods. Rather than being bases of solid community feeling, they witnessed high rates of population turnover, continued identification by large numbers of migrants with the areas from which they came, and institutional provision firmly controlled by a middle-class elite.

THE RISE OF THE WORKING-CLASS NEIGHBOURHOOD, 1880–1920

The 1880s were a vital epoch in redefining middle-class attitudes to urban space. The decade witnessed growing middle-class insecurity about the strength of their hold on the city, especially in London. Stedman Jones (1971) has shown that the 1880s saw growing concern about the degeneration of workers in the poor areas of east London, and a growing recognition that slum communities were forming over which they had virtually no control. A major outbreak of rioting by unemployed workers in the West End in 1885 heightened concern. Walkowitz (1992) has illuminated the gendered contours of this cultural crisis. Particularly troubling was the growing presence of women, sometimes prostitutes, in the urban sphere, and the fears this provoked that class boundaries would be crossed, and middle-class purity challenged. Walkowitz shows how the furore about the 'Jack-the-Ripper' murders of the late 1880s embodied such cultural disturbance, testifying to the dangers of certain urban areas.

These years hastened a middle-class re-evaluation of urban living which had begun earlier in the century. In place of the growing dangers and insecurities of the city the suburb was increasingly mooted as a realm of security and peace, in which the middle classes could live well away from the working class, while conventional gender roles could be constructed (Davidoff and Hall 1987). The middle classes began, slowly, to abdicate from the urban realm which they had created and came to favour suburban and rural living, abandoning their organising role in urban life. Although suburbanisation had begun in the early nineteenth century, it had been confined to the wealthy until the 1870s. After this period, the development of mass transport enabled a greater number of people to live away from work, and growing numbers of the lower middle class also began to live in suburbs. In London, where suburbanisation began relatively early due to the city's sheer size and the activities of property developers who built and popularised suburbs, the period between 1890 and 1914 was decisive. In 1891, 538 million journeys were made on local trains, trams and buses, a figure which rose fourfold to 2,005 million by 1914. Elsewhere, however, suburbanisation only began to have a marked impact on urban living after 1900.

Once underway, however, suburbanisation had a widespread impact. It created generally middle-class areas which formed an increasingly solid bedrock of Tory support. The first indications of a distinct Tory suburban vote can be traced to the 1870s in the south-east of England (Cornford 1963), and by the inter-war years it was a well-established feature of the political landscape. The years after 1880 saw the decline of the middle classes' civic project. They began to vacate the public stage which they had helped to create in many industrial cities as they came to identify with the privatised world of the nuclear family-dominated suburbs. Where suburbs had their own local government, the middle classes tended to lose interest in the politics of the wider city. Furthermore, as the elite middle classes moved out of the city, they left central urban spaces as working-class areas by default. Particularly important here was the fact that the lower middle class – clerks and small business people – who had previously tended to live alongside the working class, were likely to have moved to the new suburbs.

The role of industrialists in urban life was further reduced by the rise of the new limited company. Privately run firms were almost always based in a particular town and were identified with it. The coming of the joint stock company saw many firms merging with others from different districts, with the result that the control of firms often moved outside local boundaries. After 1918 many new plants were started by firms moving into a town from outside the area, especially with the first influx of American and Australian multinationals, which began to invest on a large scale in the 1930s. As a result, firms became less concerned with local politics. In the past, they had depended on the city to provide the right infrastructure for their business to flourish, and consequently they had strong incentives to get involved in local politics. After 1918, if a firm was dissatisfied with the climate in a certain town, it could move elsewhere. Although it remained rare for firms to move lock, stock and barrel from a town, it became common for them to direct new investment elsewhere, while new investors were also able to play off different local authorities in order to secure the best deal available. The result was that leading employers were less likely to be identified exclusively with specific cities, and became less concerned with the contours of local politics.

While the middle classes were losing interest in the city, working-class solidarity was growing. One important precondition for this was the maturity of the industrial city. By 1900 rates of expansion were falling, and a substantial corpus of the populations of large cities had been born and brought up within them. This gave rise to a working class with exclusive experience of urban living. The large conurbations of London, Manchester, Merseyside, the West Midlands, West Yorkshire and Tyneside were all well-established cities (Waller 1983). There were some exceptions to this trend, particularly among the smaller industrial towns and cities specialising in steel or railways, such as Barrow-in-Furness, Middlesbrough, Rotherham, Doncaster and Swindon, which had expanded very rapidly in the years after 1850. Nonetheless, the generalisation holds.

This maturity was enhanced by the fact that rates of population turnover dropped substantially. The coming of rent control in 1915 was of immense importance here, since this guaranteed rent levels to sitting tenants and provided a strong incentive for tenants to stay put. After the First World War came the development of the first large council estates (though there had been some isolated schemes from the 1870s onwards). These provided relatively good-quality housing, and since they were frequently designed for particular social groups (the early 1919 housing for the lower middle class and the 1930s housing for the working class) they led to the creation of districts with very similar types of residents.

The growing importance of the neighbourhood as a base for sociability has been underscored by studies of marriage patterns. In working-class districts McLeod (1974) has shown that towards the end of the Victorian period up to 80 per cent of marriages both bride and groom came from the same area, while the figures for middle-class neighbourhoods were only around 25 per cent. Meacham (1977), Roberts (1984), Ross (1983) and Chinn (1988) have also examined the development of strong female bonds in working-class districts at the turn of the century. As people tended to stay in one neighbourhood longer, so elaborate support networks between women were more easily facilitated. Chinn talks of the older women who would lay out dead bodies before the undertaker took over, and other women well known in the area would act as midwives or provide medical assistance. Commonly neighbours lent food and assistance to families in distress. Many women took in small-scale jobs to earn a little extra money – for instance washing, childminding and so forth, all of which depended on neighbourhood contacts at the same time as reinforcing them.

The density of contacts and the bonding of the working-class neighbourhood cannot be doubted, but the wider implications of this vibrant culture are unclear. Stedman Jones sees the new working-class culture which developed in the late nineteenth century as a form of latent consumerism, based around new commercial leisure venues, notably the music hall, which offered a 'fantasy escape from poverty' and 'no political solution to the class system' (Stedman Jones 1983: 227, 228). The songs sung in music halls said little about class divisions, but began to celebrate aristocratic, monarchical and imperialist themes. Stedman Jones's interpretation of music hall culture can, however, be challenged. Walkowitz (1992) shows that many female performers were actually intent on subtly undermining middle- and upper-class pretension, and that music hall culture contained much more latent opposition than Stedman Jones supposes. It is also important to recognise that music halls were only of marked importance in London and parts of Lancashire. Stedman Jones's figures suggest that, at their peak in the 1890s, around 45,000 people attended nightly, less than 1 per cent of London's population (Stedman Jones 1983: 205). Davies (1992: 73–74) suggests that they were of little significance in Manchester after 1918.

Many leisure venues were not commercially organised. Working men's clubs, for instance, were popular in the north and Midlands. Formed from the 1890s, they were initially controlled by middle-class patrons but increasingly came to be run by working-class men themselves, and played an important role in weakening the hold of the traditionally Tory publican on working-class social life. In 1910 there were as many as 159 clubs in Bradford, one for every 1,000 of the adult population (Jowitt 1992: 104). Furthermore, especially after 1918, the Labour movement attempted to cash in on this same trend by building Labour Clubs in many towns. Research on Preston (Savage 1987) suggests that Labour Clubs were not simply drinking dens, since membership correlated strongly with the Labour Party's electoral fortunes, implying that men and women joined out of political enthusiasm.

There is, however, the broader question of the extent to which working-class culture became commercialised in this period (see Wild 1979). An increasing amount of leisure activity depended on the transfer of monies, but it is unhelpful to regard most of it as a fully-fledged commercialism, in which private firms laid on activities simply to make profits. Gambling, for instance, largely took place in the street and bookmakers depended upon popular support and protection (Davies 1992: Chapter 6). Dance halls and cinemas were provided by small-scale entrepreneurs, many of whom would probably have come from a working-class background and remained close to their clientele. More generally, Davies (1992) argues against the idea that popular leisure was seriously affected by commercialisation in the period, and claims that informal street socialising continued to be much more important.

McKibbin has argued that the existence of an extensive neighbourhood culture meant that the institutions of the Labour movement were not organic to working-class culture:

> the development of organized hobbies, mass sport, popular betting, a modest domesticity, and commercialisation of much working-class entertainment . . . gave the working classes a certain autonomy, an opportunity to choose between alternative activities not available to any other European workforce. . . . The result was that any working-class party had to compete with an existing working-class culture which was stable and relatively sophisticated.
>
> (McKibbin 1990: 13)

The plausibility of this argument depends on the precise chronology of the maturing of the working-class neighbourhood. If, as we suggest, its rise took place relatively late, from the end of the nineteenth century, then its growth took place alongside, rather than before, the expansion of the Labour movement. In this case, the opposition between the private world of hobbies and home, and the public world of the Labour movement, might not have appeared in such stark contrast to the workers of the time.

McKibbin tends to downplay the significance of collective working-class associations, but it can be argued that these were in fact of major significance. The years after 1880 saw the Co-operative Society reaching new heights (Purvis 1990). Although retail co-operation is popularly held to have begun with the Rochdale Pioneers in 1844, it was not until the 1860s and 1870s that Co-operative Societies were established in most towns. Initially they were confined to the better-off working class since they charged higher prices and refused to allow credit, although they were ultimately cheaper than private shops since profits were returned in the annual dividend. Johnson (1985) shows that the Co-operators found it difficult to enforce their strict opposition to credit as a result of popular pressure, and they began to reach larger proportions of the urban population in the years before 1914. In 1881 they had around half a million members, but this rose to 2.1 million in

1905 and 4.6 million by 1920. Their membership, unlike that of the trade unions, continued to grow during the Depression of the 1930s, and by 1935 had reached 7.4 million members (Carr-Saunders 1938: 63). By this time, such was the level of membership in urban areas that virtually every working-class household must have had a member.

The Co-ops built shops in the city centres but also in most urban neighbourhoods, and by the 1890s posed such a threat to private retailers that some encouraged their customers to boycott them. As well as their basic retail activities, the Co-op played a major educational, social and political role. Its evening classes became important centres for both technical and general education, individual Co-ops held a variety of social events such as annual field days, and the Co-operative Women's Guild became a powerful feminist lobby.

The friendly societies dispensed basic cover for illness and old age in return for a weekly subscription. Already strong in the early nineteenth century, their numerical importance grew steadily, and by 1911 around half the adult male population paid into some sort of scheme. They also provided an important social function, with regular weekly branch meetings. Unlike the Co-ops, however, they began to decline after the introduction of national insurance in 1911. Alongside the Co-ops and friendly societies other forms of mutual self-provisioning were in evidence in some areas. South Wales, in particular, became well known for its popular building societies, when groups of workers banded together to fund the building of their own houses (Daunton 1977), and for its medical clubs, where working-class subscribers employed doctors and controlled medical services directly (Savage 1987).

Members of the working class also became more active in the institutional fabric bequeathed by the middle classes, especially the churches. There is some evidence that popular religious enthusiasm increased from the 1890s, as middle-class involvement in urban religious provision declined, and as working-class members became more active in organising church activities. In Preston – an atypical case because of the strength of the Catholic Church in the city – attendance at (Anglican and Catholic) churches increased, and the Catholics built a number of Catholic working men's clubs.

These developments testify to a changing relationship between the *petite bourgeoisie* and the working-class community. In the mid-nineteenth century, small traders and shopkeepers had played a pivotal role within the working-class neighbourhood as purveyors of services and amenities to unstable and shifting populations. As time went on, however, their relationship changed. Retailers, threatened by the rise of the multiple store such as Boots and W.H. Smith, as well as by the Co-op, formed associations and developed a stronger corporate sense of identity, and in the process distanced themselves from their clientele. Publicans, under threat from Liberal legislation as well as the rise of registered drinking clubs (such as working men's clubs), increasingly leant towards the Tories at the same time as their customers were abandoning whatever Tory allegiance they had once possessed.

One of the most important features of the new working-class institutions was that while based in neighbourhood life they reached out from it and encompassed the wider urban realm. Many of the institutions were organised at the urban, rather than the neighbourhood, level. This applies to the Co-op, the friendly societies (who frequently organised a friendly societies council for each town) and the local trades unions (in their trades councils). By the First World War the decline of elite middle-class civic involvement and the rise of working-class associational activity had turned many towns and cities from middle-class to working-class environments. The process was, of course, uneven. In general it took place earlier in the smaller industrial towns, while elite involvement in larger cities continued longer. The city of Birmingham, where the Chamberlain family remained dominant in local politics down to the Second World War, is a case in point. But, while the process was not unilinear, the general trends were clear.

URBAN CHANGE AFTER 1914

The 'golden years' of the working-class city were few. From as early as the first decade of the twentieth century, forces were in action which would undermine the vitality of the urban arena. Yet these forces were slow to become effective, and in the first three decades of the twentieth century the industrial cities became a productive base on which working-class solidarity could build.

In the years after 1900 the expansion of local authority intervention seemed to mark a new era for city living. As Stevenson has noted, 'the period from the late nineteenth century to the Second World War might well be called the heyday of local government' (Stevenson 1984: 307). The First World War saw a dramatic extension of municipal action as councils organised an increasing number of local services, including food supply, medical services, and the relief of the poor and refugees. In many areas the period marked the first serious attempt to co-opt the Labour movement into municipal administration, and it was the prelude to the dramatic expansion of municipal activity in the years after 1918, an expansion in which local Labour movements played a key role.

After 1918 municipal activity increased extensively in the provision of medical care and education. Local authorities became more involved in the provision of hospitals (especially after the transfer of Poor Law responsibilities to the local authorities in 1929), and they also provided facilities for maternity and child health and the control of infectious diseases. They were increasingly active in the provision of amenities such as water, gas and electricity, in many cases taking control of local facilities from private companies. Educational provision improved, especially in secondary schools, where the number of places more than doubled between 1914 and 1938, the resources for this expansion coming overwhelmingly from local pockets. Although central government spending on education rose dramatically during the First World War, levels were cut back after the mid-1920s, and the cost of improving educational facilities fell on the local authorities, whose spending rose from £24 million in 1919/20 to £47 million by 1937/38 (Stevenson 1984: 248ff.).

This expansion in local government responsibilities meant that total local authority spending rose from £140 million in 1913 to £533 million in 1939. As we discuss in greater detail in the next chapter, this expansion was related to the growing desire of local Labour Parties to develop municipal services, so that Labour became a party increasingly identified with the provision of urban public services – a trend which marked a major reversal of their pre-war scepticism about the role of public intervention.

Yet, in the very years that the development of public services seemed to indicate that a new era of urban glory was approaching, other pressures began to lead in other directions. The most important development was the massively expanded role of the councils in the provision of housing, as parliamentary legislation from 1919 gave councils the ability to build with generous subsidies. Over a million council houses were built between the wars, and the proportion of municipal housing rose from 1 per cent in 1913 to 13 per cent in 1947. The same period also saw a dramatic rise in speculative building for owner occupation, especially on suburban sites, though this was heavily focused in the south-east of England (excluding London), where 92 per cent of all new completions were carried out by the private sector between 1919 and 1940. As Dickens *et al.* (1985) have shown, high rates of council house building (given the size of population) were heavily concentrated in the working-class areas of the north and Midlands, with Northumberland, South and East Yorkshire,

Staffordshire, Worcestershire and Cambridgeshire being especially prominent (Dickens *et al*. 1985: Figure 5.1b).

These new housing developments were to enhance and intensify the pressures towards suburbanisation which were already under way. Strongly influenced by the concept of the 'garden city', most early council housing was designed for suburban locations, and for those on a good income: it was not until 1933 that serious attempts were made to provide housing for poor urban dwellers. Pooley and Irish (1987) have shown that in the inter-war years it became possible for the skilled working class to move to private and public suburban estates, so beginning a process of working-class dispersal from the city which was to gather pace over time. On Merseyside around 53 per cent of those in private suburban housing, and between 41 per cent and 50 per cent of those in public suburban housing, were from the skilled working class.

From the later 1920s a fresh and profound wave of migration also led to a considerable movement of workers from old-established industrial areas to new expanding towns in which new solidarities had to be forged. New urban areas in the Midlands and south grew quickly. Boom towns such as Coventry, Oxford, Luton, Slough and the outer London fringe saw growth. In the most remarkable case, Slough increased from 7,400 inhabitants in 1901 to 60,000 by 1938. The onset of the 1929 slump led to severe unemployment in the old traditional industries, and a steady stream of people moved from Wales and the north-east to the more buoyant areas of the south and Midlands. Altogether around one million people moved into the south-east between 1921 and 1935 (Owen 1937).

The implications of this major population movement on working-class community ties in the new areas is uncertain. Much initial migration was speculative. Rather than being migration into a city in which a relative or friend was already living, people moved because they had heard that jobs were available. Of migrants to Oxford 75 per cent were unmarried (Daniel 1939). However, over time, it seems that relatives did move to join their kin, and by 1937 46 out of 60 migrants interviewed were moving to be near family members. Therefore, although there is some evidence that new community ties did form, the conclusion seems unavoidable that migration was disruptive in the short term. And, although Zeitlin (1980) claims that the Welsh were able to bring their trade union traditions to the Midlands, in fact the unions found it very difficult to establish themselves in these new industrial areas (Savage 1988b).

A considerable proportion of migration was organised through state transference schemes, which allowed young boys (and a few young girls) from the depressed areas to be relocated in the more buoyant areas. The state paid for the fare of the workers, and helped them with lodging and pocket money until they found a job. Between 1929 and 1936, 242,049 workers had been moved, perhaps a quarter of total migrants. The Ministry of Labour also provided training centres which allowed young workers to learn new skills.

What was clear from these population movements was that the social topography of the Victorian industrial city was being redrawn. Population decline in city centres began as early as the mid-Victorian period. The creation of London's railway stations led to a massive exodus of residents (Stedman Jones 1971). Until the turn of the century, however, most of those who left tended to move to nearby areas. From 1900, decline began in earnest. The central areas of Finsbury, Holborn and the City of London lost 10 per cent of their population or more between 1911 and 1921 as people moved to outer London. The Lancashire textile towns of Blackburn, Burnley, Bury, Oldham and Rochdale were also recording small population losses in the period.

It was not until the 1920s that these exceptional areas were joined by others, principally a number of shipbuilding and coal towns. However, the turning point was the 1930s, the period in which many large conurbations fell into decline. The contraction of population in central London reached astonishing proportions. Between 1911 and 1951 six boroughs saw their population fall by over half. Shoreditch and Finsbury lost no less than 60 per cent, Stepney 65 per cent. Poplar, the site of one of the most vibrant neighbourhood cultures (Rose 1989), experienced a 54 per cent reduction. The same process, albeit on a less dramatic scale, affected Manchester, Liverpool and parts of the West Midlands.

There was more to this trend than the movement of population. Working-class communities were never the static, unchanging entities reflected in some accounts, and internal tensions also played their part in leading people to question traditional forms of urban living. Generational and gender tensions were especially important. A number of writers have shown that it was working-class women who played a leading role in redefining urban living. Mark-Lawson *et al.* (1985) have pointed to the importance of women's struggles in securing the extension of municipal provision. Davies (1992) has noted that it was women who were particularly attracted to the new urban leisure pursuit of cinema going. And it was women, according to White's (1986) study of a slum neighbourhood in Islington, who were most active in undermining the slum culture by moving to better areas.

CONCLUSIONS

Seen in this more dynamic framework, the first three decades of the century seem even more remarkable as the period after the departure of elite middle-class influence from the cities and before the decline of urban centres brought about by continued suburbanisation. The period saw the city become increasingly identified with the working class, which developed a distinct urban territorial base. The maturing of the industrial city was crucial to the formation of the working class.

However, it is also necessary to be attuned to the specific processes occurring in different cities. The process of urban class formation might take place differently in different cities, according to specific cultural traditions or local social relations. In newer industrial towns, for instance in the south-east of England, where migrants were new and neighbourhoods unsettled, working-class formation was inhibited. In some older cities elite members fought hard to retain a strong urban presence: the best example – the Chamberlains in Birmingham – has already been mentioned. In some places such as Liverpool, Manchester and parts of London, differences between Irish and English workers proved to be especially divisive (Fielding 1993), even though in comparative perspective such divisions were less intense than in other countries such as the United States. It appears to be the case that working-class cultures became most robust and militant in those cities where there was a powerful working associational life based in specific neighbourhoods (see also Hobsbawm 1987), but also where there were vibrant activities at the wider urban level. On Clydeside for instance, a confrontational working class was well organised in specific areas, but was also able to mobilise on a wider scale.

5 Working-class politics

In the previous chapters we have shown, on the basis of an expanded conception of what class formation involves, that the period under consideration was decisive in shaping the working class. Changes in the economic sphere, but also, crucially, in the wider set of social relations defined by social mobility and urban change, assisted and encouraged this process. However, the process of class formation, as has been stressed throughout, was dynamic, complex and contingent. It was neither smooth, nor unambiguous, nor predictable. Countervailing tendencies persisted, particularly in the realm of gender relations.

In this chapter we consider the political implications of class formation, in order to show how the changes we have discussed in the earlier chapters of this book affected political alignments. We begin by examining recent revisionist claims concerning the weakness of the Labour Party for much of the twentieth century. We argue that although these accounts usefully draw attention to some of the weaknesses of the Labour movement, the rise of the Labour Party was still an event of considerable historical importance. The rest of the chapter shows how the strengths and weaknesses of the Labour movement can be related to the specific character of working-class formation which we have discussed in earlier chapters. In what follows our analysis focuses on four crucial developments discussed above: first, the declining salience of the skill division within the male working class; second, the threat to the traditional patriarchal authority of the working-class male posed by the decline of the informal labour market, the substitution of men's labour by women's, and the ambiguous role of women in the urban realm; third, the bureaucratisation of the labour market and its consequent 'politicisation'; finally the process of urban class formation and the growing identification of urban space with the working class.

We are not claiming that these changes determined political change in any simple manner. Because class formation was complex, contradictory and open to interpretation, so political parties had considerable discretion in how – or if – they mobilised. Indeed, at times there were contradictory effects. It proved difficult for political parties to appeal both to working-class men threatened by women's economic activity and to women themselves. The subsequent analysis will therefore show how the unevenness of the Labour Party's history was due to the difficulty it faced in articulating all these developments, and how other political parties could also attempt to mobilise on these axes.

THE NEW REVISIONISM: HISTORIANS AND THE LABOUR PARTY

As we showed in Chapter 1, early labour historians regarded the rise of the Labour Party in the first part of the twentieth century as a dramatic event, which marked the entry of the working class into the political arena, and thereby signalled the development of a new socialist politics. In more recent years, however, historians have become more sceptical about the extent to which the rise of Labour marked a fundamental change in political alignments and cultures, and have tended instead to emphasise continuities in political history.

Revisionists claim that there is no reason to suppose that the working class is necessarily attracted to Labour politics. They stress that the working class has often been politically active outside the Labour movement, and that there is no reason to suppose that the Liberal and Conservative Parties could not successfully respond to, and even articulate, working-class political demands. A good example of this view is P.F. Clarke's (1971) claim that in the period between 1900 and 1914 the Liberal Party became committed to a 'New Liberalism' in which it attempted to devise a politics which would appeal to working-class voters, so reducing its appeal to traditional 'status groups' (such as religious groupings). Clarke argues that the success of the Liberals in the elections of 1906 and 1910, when they promised a series of social reforms and launched a major offensive against land-owning and plutocratic interests, was testimony to the electoral viability of their strategy. More recently Clarke's views have in large part been endorsed by Tanner (1990), who claims that the early Labour movement was rarely able to break the hold of Liberalism over working-class voters before 1914. In a detailed study of local politics in various parts of Britain, Tanner concludes that only in a few areas – usually where the Liberals were already weak – was the Labour movement able to become a real political force before the First World War.

Other historians have stressed the ability of the Conservative Party to appeal to the working class. The strength of popular Toryism in the later nineteenth century, especially in industrial Lancashire, has been demonstrated by Joyce (1980). Joyce claims that working-class Toryism was based around deference to local employers, but this does not seem convincing because these same workers also engaged in non-deferential behaviour such as joining trade unions and going on strike. Savage (1987) and Lawrence (1991) have argued that the Tories owed their success to their ability to appeal to working-class economic interests, for instance by encouraging firms to set up and provide employment. In the period after 1900 it was the Tories who led the way in adjusting to the democratic franchise by providing a range of popular bodies and institutions to garner electoral support. The Primrose League was the first serious political initiative directed at women voters, and the Tories built Conservative working men's clubs and developed strong ward organisations (Pugh 1985). As proof of the success of the Tories in adapting to the modern political system, McKibbin (1990) has shown that Britain was unusual among western nations in seeing a right-wing party as the main party of government for most of the inter-war years: in eighteen out of the twenty-one years between the wars the Conservatives (albeit often in coalition) were in office.

Finally, it has been argued that the rise of the Labour Party did not in itself mark a fundamental departure from the principles and aims of Liberalism. During the Liberal government of 1906 the twenty-nine Labour MPs found it difficult to distinguish their politics from those of that administration. Stedman Jones (1983) claimed that the Labour Party took over many of the 'progressive' assumptions of Liberalism, and gained most electoral support when it won the votes of significant proportions of the middle classes. But Liberals have always been non-socialist; it cannot be denied that there have always been notable socialist elements within the Labour Party (especially those organised through the Independent Labour Party), and that Labour adopted a socialist constitution in 1918. It is unclear, however, whether such socialist views were endorsed by working-class voters, and in practice the policies of the Labour governments of 1924 and 1929 (handicapped though they were by being minority administrations) showed little evidence of commitment to socialism. Even in those areas such as 'Red Clydeside' which have traditionally been seen as marked by intense socialist agitation (Hinton 1973), more recent historians such as Iain

MacLean (1983) have argued that the vast majority of Labour voters were not influenced by Marxist firebrands such as John Maclean or Willy Gallacher. MacLean argues that Labour owed its strength in the area largely to the solid Irish Catholic support it gathered in the years after 1922. Reid (1985) has endorsed these claims, arguing that the rise of the Labour Party was not due to any enthusiasm for socialist politics, or to the development of a more militant or united working class. Rather, he claims, it was related to a recognition by trade unionists during the First World War that state intervention could help support trade unions and working-class demands more generally. In other words, the growth of Labour did not mark a fundamental break from older patterns of trade union loyalties and sectionalism, but simply their continuation under another guise.

This body of recent literature offers a powerful challenge to the historical significance of the rise of Labour. It emphasises that political change cannot be seen as a simple reflex of socio-economic mutation. Political parties are not passive products of social change. They can devise policies and appeals which may be effective at constructing support, and by this process cause, as much as respond to, social and economic change. It is important, however, not to throw the baby out with the bathwater. Just because workers have never unanimously supported a progressive socialist politics does not disprove the existence or influence of class. Political parties have to work on a broad terrain in which class and other social influences have a profound effect, as we now want to show.

THE RISE OF LABOUR, 1880–1918

It is extremely rare for a new political party to become a party of government in less than a quarter of a century, and to retain its prominent position thereafter. Formed in 1900 (as the Labour Representation Committee), the Labour Party displaced the Liberals as the second party in 1918 and formed its first (albeit minority) government in 1924. Labour is the only 'third party' ever to make a successful challenge to one of the two erstwhile dominant parties in the British political arena. Although the SDP/Liberal alliance came close to reversing this process in 1983, the Labour Party is the only party which can truly lay claim to having 'broken the mould' of British politics since the development of party alignments in the seventeenth century (see Figure 5.1).

Moreover, comparative research shows that it is unusual, though not impossible, for a new party to become a major political force without fundamental constitutional upheaval. Admittedly, it has been argued by Matthew *et al.* (1976) that the rise of Labour after 1918 was in fact due to constitutional change, more specifically to the enfranchisement of large numbers of working-class men and women who had been excluded from earlier extensions of the franchise in 1867 and 1884. However, Tanner's (1990) research shows that the working class was the clear majority of the electorate even before 1918, and that the main effect of the 1918 reform was to enfranchise women and young men of all classes. In short, it cannot be denied that the rise of the British Labour Party was a remarkable feat that represented a major shift of political opinion away from the Liberal Party.

Figure 5.1   Labour's electoral support, 1900–1983

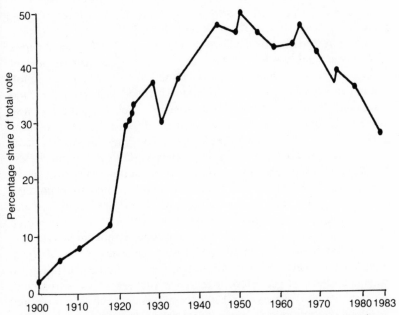

Source: A.H. Halsey (1986), *Change in British Society,* Oxford: Oxford University Press.

This is no small achievement. However, we wish to distance ourselves from any heroic interpretation of the rise of the Labour Party which is implied by the metaphor of the 'Forward March of Labour' (Hobsbawm 1981). In particular, it is all too easy to read contemporary political agendas into the early Labour Party, and then to rewrite the history of the party as the gradual elaboration of these. Rather than being a linear development, the history of the Labour Party has been subject to major redefinition and discontinuity as it sought to establish and consolidate on shifting and at times contradictory social bases.

The early Labour Party developed largely as a defensive reaction by trade unionists to the loss of autonomy and control which were brought about by the changes to the labour market discussed in Chapter 3. As Thane (1985) and Pelling (1968) have shown, the early Labour movement was generally not interested in social reform brought about by the state, except for reforms (such as the provision of old age pensions or meals for school children) which largely affected those outside the labour market. In fact, as Tanner (1990) shows, it was the Liberals who frequently took the lead here. In those areas such as London or Glasgow where the Labour movement was more radical and supported more ambitious forms of 'municipal socialism', there were often very strong Liberal traditions (Smith 1984) and a strong culture of 'Progressivism' which they could draw on (Thane 1991).

Labour rested its appeal before 1914 on its narrowly defined defence of the 'trade union interest', both at local level (through support of clauses demanding that the local council should use trade union labour) and at national level (in demands for legal protection for trade unionism). This was precisely the area in which the Liberals were suspect. Trade unionists were wary of the Liberals' commitment to trade unionism since large employers, sometimes known for their personal hostility to trade unionism, were still active in Liberal circles. Furthermore 'New Liberalism' embodied an attempt to use the state to protect individual wellbeing, and remained attached to a political philosophy concerned with dealing with individual characteristics rather than social relations. Its main social reforms, such as national insurance and old age pensions, provided state support to individuals, and can be seen as an attempt to construct a new form of social citizenship in which the private person was entitled to certain minimum standards of provision. It therefore had few ideas as to how to deal with issues concerned with class relations between employers and workers. For this reason, many of its demands, while in many cases attractive to workers on their own terms, simply did not address the sort of class issues which they knew to be vitally important to them. Furthermore, as we have seen, the Liberals' social reforms endorsed the sort of bureaucratisation which undercut traditional working practices, so encouraging the development of a defensive trade union politics. In short, the Liberal success of the immediate pre-war years also helped to produce, in its wake, a powerful impetus for trade union politicisation which might threaten Liberal dominance.

It is a little misleading to characterise Labour politics before 1914 simply in terms of defensiveness. This attitude was forcefully challenged by many socialist groups, notably the Independent Labour Party (ILP). It is only in the past few years that historians such as Howell (1983), McKinlay and Morris (1991), and James *et al.* (1992) have shown that the ILP was a party in its own right, not just a small branch of the Labour Party. Although it never had more than 20,000 members (Laybourn 1992), in some places, such as Glasgow, Bradford and Leicester (Lancaster 1987), the ILP became the dominant political force in local Labour politics, and pressed strongly for municipal provision of local services. The ILP did best in small towns with stable populations. Yet as Howell (1983) emphasises, while the ILP was avowedly socialist, it found it difficult to shake off the political mantle of radical Liberalism. Furthermore some of the ILP's politics shared in the reactionary currents which had a wider audience in the Labour movement. Hannam (1992) has shown that while the ILP appeared to be an important supporter of women's struggles (especially women's suffrage), it endorsed a politics in which women were defined as mothers and wives, rather than as independent workers in their own right.

The Labour movement had therefore developed a distinct political presence before 1914. Although Tanner (1990) has emphasised the success of the Liberals in containing the challenge from Labour, they had not managed to prevent the articulation of a legitimate 'labour interest' which proclaimed the need for independent political representation. What was in doubt in 1914 was whether the Labour Party would be able to become a party of government, or whether it would remain a minority party looking after specific, narrowly defined, trade union interests, leaving the Liberals and Tories to contest effective parliamentary power. Between 1910 and 1914 Labour did not do well electorally, floundering in most by-elections and even losing some municipal council seats it had gained in earlier years (Adams 1990; Shepherd and Halstead 1979; Tanner 1990). Yet, while the Liberals were able to contain the Labour movement, they could not absorb it. After the defection of the mining union MPs to the Labour Party in 1908 trade unions no longer sought political influence through the Liberals. The Liberals' inability to articulate a politics recognising the different interests of capital and labour forced the trade unions to demand independent representation.

THE MOMENT OF TRADE UNION MILITANCY, 1910–1926

The fact that Labour originated as a trade union party is hardly in doubt: it has been a central claim of traditional labour history for many years (e.g. Pelling 1965). However, while the Labour Party began as a defensive movement of trade unionists representing skilled male workers, there are strong grounds for arguing that after the First World War this became a much less significant dimension of its electoral support and growth (though not of its finances or its personnel), and that the crucial factor behind the consolidation of the Labour Party lay in its growing role as an urban party able to draw upon the neighbourhood bases of support and loyalty identified in Chapter 4.

This process was, however, a complex one. In the years after 1910 there was a sudden escalation of workplace conflict, which appeared to be the crux of political change. The years between 1910 and 1914 saw major disputes in the mining, textile and transport sectors, mainly caused by the fall in real wages. What was notable about this industrial unrest compared to previous strikes was the extent to which it was the result of unofficial shopfloor campaigns. Some activists even began to campaign for a 'general strike'. Hinton (1973), Cronin (1984), Burgess (1980) and Price (1980) have all argued that the First World War saw an accentuation of workplace conflict between capital and labour, with the state playing an important role by becoming actively involved in regulating industry, undermining established working practices and keeping wages down. The tensions caused by this situation led to an explosion of industrial unrest from the latter half of the war until the early 1920s, especially as wages failed to keep pace with soaring inflation. Trade union membership grew to unprecedented heights, and by 1920 half the workforce was unionised. Throughout the early 1920s crisis prevailed, as the government attempted to reduce its regulatory role in industry, and was forced to take on a trade union movement hostile to the resurgence of private enterprise this entailed. Despite some notable successes, the trade union movement slowly lost ground as the state abandoned its interest in a corporate approach to economic management. In 1926 the General Strike saw many workers come out in support of the miners who were fighting wage reductions, but the defeat which came with the Trade Union Congress's capitulation marked the end of the period of militant trade unionism.

What was remarkable about these conflicts was the leading role of the new 'industrial' trade unions of semi-skilled and unskilled workers. This testified to the fact that the axis of skill was of far less significance than before 1910. As we have seen in Chapter 2, the skill divide was of steadily decreasing significance within the working class, and one of the main impacts of the war was to bring about a growing uniformity of wages among workers. In the years after 1918 it was the semi-skilled workers organised in the National Union of Railwaymen, the Transport and General Workers Union and the National Union of Mineworkers who played the leading role in trade unionism. Of particular note was the development of alliances between trade unions and a new work solidarity which transcended particular occupations and trades. The General Strike of 1926, in which hundreds of thousands of workers went on strike in sympathy with the miners, and in which very few workers who were called out refused to comply, was a notable example of this new solidarity. Fifty years previously when the skilled and unskilled working class enjoyed such limited association it would have been unimaginable.

Nonetheless, despite the impressive male working-class unity demonstrated by post-First World War events, it is still not clear that these struggles had a major impact on the fortunes of the Labour Party itself. There are a number of problems in explaining popular support for the Labour Party simply in terms of fall-out from the workplace conflicts and trade union movements discussed above. There is first a problem of chronology. Labour's electoral support peaked in the later 1920s when trade union membership was falling, and was actually rather poor in 1918 when workplace conflict was at its height. Adams (1990) has also shown that there is no general association between specific occupational experience and the rise of the Labour vote in the early post-war period. Some dock areas in the East End of London and Hull swung very heavily to Labour, while others in Liverpool and Cardiff did not. Adams also shows that there were strong swings to Labour in some industries, such as Sheffield's cutlery industry, which had not seen marked industrial conflict or wartime state intervention.

There is also a problem of showing any clear general association between trade union membership and Labour Party support. Detailed surveys have only been carried out since the 1960s, well after the period which interests us, but it is suggestive that they show that trade union membership does not correlate with voting Labour (Franklin 1985). From 1927, when trade union members had to 'contract in' to pay financial contributions to the Labour Party, around 51 per cent did so. Some unions, such as the miners', where the association between trade unionism and political activity is unusually clear, saw very high proportions paying contributions to the Labour Party, but others, such as the engineers' union (the AEU), saw only 24 per cent pay such dues. In short, there were plenty of trade unionists who were not committed enough to Labour to donate any money to it.

One of the problems was that trade unionism continued to be divisive. This was especially true in relations between male and female workers. The introduction of women into many workplaces during the First World War, as well as the longer-term trend discussed in Chapters 2 and 3 for men to be displaced by women, led many trade unions to campaign forcibly for the exclusion of women from the workplace during the war and directly afterwards. This was hardly an attitude designed to appeal to those newly enfranchised women voters who had experienced wartime freedoms brought about by relatively high wages, and had no wish to relinquish them.

In retrospect, while workplace militancy between 1917 and the mid-1920s was testimony to the development of a much more homogeneous male working class, it continued to reflect the concerns of a defensive trade union movement endeavouring to restore a traditional status quo. Far from embracing state intervention, as Reid (1985) suggests, the Labour movement continued to regard the state with suspicion (Adams 1990). Admittedly, at times defensiveness might give way to quite innovative ideas about how workers' control and autonomy could be reconstructed. Some workers championed guild socialism and syndicalism which argued for direct worker self-management, while other socialists were more attracted to state control of industry through nationalisation. Yet what was lacking from these movements was a sense of politics and identity outside the workplace, a politics of service provision and consumption, a politics which might particularly appeal to women.

Therefore, one of the characteristics of Labour in the 1920s was the extent to which the instability of its trade union support led it to seek backing in the working-class urban areas which had emerged in the previous few decades. The association between Labour and the industrial working-class town was to become of major importance, and helped to define it as a party which increasingly became identified with municipal services and state intervention. However, the process by which Labour became identified with the provision of local authority services was not a straightforward one (Howard 1983). It owed something to a long-standing, pre-war tradition of municipal socialism associated with the ILP. In the early 1920s municipal socialism reached new heights with 'Poplarism'. Here, councillors in the London Borough of Poplar insisted on high levels of Poor Law benefit in a period of high unemployment, and demanded that they be subsidised by the richer London boroughs. Eventually, however, Labour councillors were imprisoned and the protest collapsed, while the national Labour Party refused to support the movement.

In most areas, however, Labour was reluctant to take an active municipal role in the early 1920s. The reasons for this lay partly in the persistence of trade union influence within local parties, which frequently accepted the need for financial orthodoxy in the running of local budgets, and partly in fears that illegal political action would bring the Labour Party itself into disrepute, as had happened in Poplar. Indeed, the course adopted by Poplar's neighbour, Hackney, was of greater long-term impact. Here the Labour Mayor, Herbert Morrison, presided over a Labour council wedded to legality and due procedure (Donoughue and Jones 1973).

As a consequence of the collapse in membership in the 1920s, trade union control at the local level began to fade over the course of the decade. Haltingly, local Labour Parties realised in the early 1920s that the road to political power would be long and hard. Before 1918 it had been the Tories who were the prime innovators in developing forms of popular neighbourhood organisation, and most local Labour Parties had made only limited attempts to build up ward organisation and a genuine presence in working-class neighbourhoods – though there were notable exceptions to this, such as the Woolwich Labour Party. In the early 1920s, Labour performed disappointingly in local elections (after an excellent showing in 1919), and it attempted to remedy this by building up ward activity and placing greater emphasis on recruiting individual members and using them to organise local campaigning. Some historians have questioned the success of this shift (Howard 1983), but it is worth recognising that 400,000 individual members were recruited by 1930, and Savage (1987) shows that Labour frequently did best where these ward organisations were strongest.

This shift to ward activity permitted working-class women to have greater influence over the party. Women were particularly interested in expanding local authority services since they were the constituency most neglected by the mutual self-help initiatives characteristic of the period before 1914. Friendly society and trade union benefits were geared towards male wage earners, and female housewives were not covered by their sickness benefits. As Mark-Lawson *et al.* (1985) have shown, it was where women were best organised that the Labour Party became converted to the politics of state welfare (see also Savage 1990). Women, either organised through the Independent Labour Party or in the women's sections of the Labour Party, became the strongest advocates of the provision of nursery education, improved health care for mothers and children, and so forth. The significance of women's involvement in the inter-war Labour Parties is rarely appreciated, but the figures are impressive. There were around 200,000 members of the women's section in the mid-1920s, and 155,000 individual women members in 1933, about 40 per cent of the total individual membership.

Labour was also pushed into the camp of defending public services because opposition to the party at local level became increasingly focused on 'ratepayer' interests. As we showed in Chapter 4, the leading force pressing for municipal intervention in the period before 1914, large industrialists, had largely retired from the stage, leaving political action to small business people and professionals (Hennock 1973). In many cases these sorts of groups were reluctant to press for municipal development because of their traditional hostility to high rates (though there were exceptions to this), and energy for development had to flow through the Labour movement, if only by default.

Labour's association with urban local government can also be attributed to its desire to establish itself as the legitimate working-class party. In the post-Second World War period Labour appeared to be the only left-wing party in British politics and it is easy to assume that this had always been the case. However, the situation was much more confused after the First World War. In the 1920s Labour was challenged by the Communist Party, which despite its small membership and limited electoral support had a dedicated core of activists and exercised an influence out of all proportion to its numbers. In 1931 the disaffiliation of the ILP from the Labour Party also caused concern as it sought to develop an independent electoral base, with some success in its strongholds. The Labour Party needed to establish itself over its left-wing rivals as the legitimate working-class party in Britain. By becoming an established party of local government Labour could present itself as the only effective opposition to the established parties, and could thereby distance itself from its left-wing opponents.

Another factor making Labour an urban party was its erratic general election performance. From only fifty-five seats in 1918, it grew extremely fast in the 1920s, forming governments in 1924 and in 1929 when it obtained 287 seats. Following the capitulation of the Labour government in the face of Treasury pressure to cut public spending, and the departure of Ramsay MacDonald to head a National Government, it only won a miserly fifty-two seats in 1931. A partial recovery was then achieved in the 1935 election when 151 Labour MPs were returned. By contrast, the Party's municipal progress was rather more steady and sure. It won control of a few city councils in the 1920s (Leeds, Hull, Swansea, Barnsley and Blackburn), and in the early 1930s it took control of the large urban councils of London, Glasgow and Sheffield, together with a number of other smaller cities (Cook

1975). From the late 1920s Labour regularly polled a much higher proportion of the municipal vote than any other party – for instance, in 1935 46 per cent, compared to 27 per cent for the Tories, 8 per cent for the Liberals and 20 per cent for Independents (Stevenson and Cook 1979: 289). In the dark years after 1931 Labour activists could take comfort in the fact that the party seemed inexorably to be rising to predominate in urban local government. Labour could begin to use its local experience as a political platform both to develop policy, and to advertise its achievements to the electorate.

More than anyone else Herbert Morrison was the architect of this new Labour politics (Donoughue and Jones 1973). Morrison was an emblem of Labour's inter-war fortunes. In the early 1920s he became an influential figure in Hackney Council. In the mid-1920s he became a Labour MP and was appointed Minister of Transport in the 1929 government. During this period, as Secretary of the London Labour Party, he built up a Labour electoral machine throughout the city. Following the loss of his seat in 1931, he became leader of London County Council in 1934, an office in which he celebrated his distinct new vision of Labour politics. From a lower middle-class background, he regarded trade unions with suspicion, so distancing himself from the trade union wing of the party. He articulated a new politics of consumption, geared to showing how Labour could provide the most efficient services to urban consumers, especially in the fields of transport, housing and health. His vision was to show that municipal services were more competent than private companies, and therefore that Labour could win support not as a trade union party but as a party of efficient local government.

This idea was not unique to London. The failures of industrial struggle in the 1920s and the growing interest by women and ward activists in local authority politics led to a greater articulation of consumer demands within local Labour politics which enhanced the development of the party's distinctly urban role. Table 5.1 shows that in 1918 Labour's strength was located predominantly outside the large cities. Only 19 per cent of its small number of MPs, and 22 per cent of its total vote, were drawn from the large cities, with the majority coming from smaller towns where it had built up support before the First World War, and especially in the mining districts. Only Manchester, where Labour won four seats, was a Labour stronghold in 1918. However, eleven years later, by 1929, this pattern had shifted. In this election, which saw Labour reaching its inter-war peak of popularity, it won nearly two-thirds of the large urban seats and these accounted for 40 per cent of its total number of MPs. In every city bar Liverpool

Labour won at least half the seats and large cities accounted for almost one-third of its total vote. As Labour fell back following its debacle in 1931, it was forced into its heartlands, which now tended to be the large urban areas. Admittedly in 1935 Labour did not do as well as it had hoped in the cities, especially in the West Midlands and to some extent in the north-east, while its vote increased significantly in rural and suburban areas (Stevenson and Cook 1979). However, its areas of strength were still predominantly urban: in 1935 42 per cent of its MPs were drawn from the large cities, a higher proportion than before.

Table 5.1   Labour and the large cities,* 1919–1945

City	Number of Labour MPs			Total seats
	1918	*1928*	*1935*	
London	2	36	22	61
London County Boroughs	0	13	10	24
Glasgow	1	10	9	15
Manchester/Salford	4	8	4	13
Birmingham	0	6	0	12
Liverpool	0	5	3	12
Sheffield	0	5	4	7
Leeds	1	4	2	6
Bristol	0	4	2	5
Edinburgh	1	3	1	5
Bradford	0	4	1	4
Kingston upon Hull	0	3	2	4
Newcastle	0	2	0	4
Nottingham	1	2	1	4
Potteries	1	4	4	4
All large cities	11	115	65	180
Large city MPs as a percentage of all Labour MPs	19	40	43	28**

Source: Calculated from F.W.S. Craig (1977), *British Parliamentary Election Results 1918–1949*, London: Macmillan.

*'Large city' defined as having four or more constituencies
**Large city seats as a percentage of all seats in the House of Commons

REVERSAL AND RETREAT, 1931–1942

Labour consolidated its position as one of the two leading political parties in Britain in the 1930s, and despite its inability to shake the hold of the Conservative-led National Government, it stood as the main opposition to it. Yet McKibbin (1990) is correct to point to the very real limitations of the Labour Party in attracting working-class support. It never attracted more than 37 per cent of the total vote, and even if we assume that this vote was entirely a working-class one, and that the middle classes voted for other parties, we are still left with the inescapable conclusion that more working-class people voted against Labour than for it.

Labour's weakness was multi-faceted. In part it stemmed from the manifest failure of the 1929 Labour government, and the ensuing disappointment. Also, the support of women, which had been crucial in the run-up to the election, was compromised, especially in areas where women had a strong labour market presence, by the Labour government's decision to restrict married women's eligibility for unemployment benefit. And although the rise of mass unemployment did not divide the working class, it was a signal example of the failure of the Labour government to improve living conditions.

Beyond this, the Labour Party was increasingly confronted by problems of identity in the inter-war years. The more successful it became as a working-class party, and the more distinctive its appeal as an urban party, the less it was able to present itself as a 'national' party which transcended and resolved particular sectional interests. In this sense, Labour's strengths were also its weaknesses. For much of the nineteenth century there was little association between political dissent and urbanism. There were, in fact, strong traditions of rural protest, encapsulated in intermittent waves of agrarian trade unionism, religious dissent and Liberal politics, while many large cities proved inhospitable to radical politics. Indeed, many early socialists, such as Allen Clarke and Robert Blatchford, regarded cities as the ultimate capitalist evil and emphasised the need for socialists to reappropriate the countryside. Yet the trend for Labour to become a distinctly urban party made it more difficult to cater to those people whose dream was to move out of the city. This problem was exacerbated by a parallel process of cultural reconstruction beginning in the later nineteenth century, whereby it was rural traditions which became valued as quintessential components of 'Englishness' (Weiner 1981). Labour, however, was weak in those very places which came to be identified with national sentiments, making it more difficult to represent itself as a 'national' party. A further illuminating illustration of this point is

Labour's poor performance in towns closely associated with defence, such as Portsmouth (see Stevenson and Cook 1979: 252, 255).

Furthermore, as we have seen in Chapter 4, just as Labour was coming to be defined as an urban party, so in many cases industrial cities themselves were beginning to decline. Labour in the 1930s was the party of old and decaying places, rather than the new and dynamic ones. Labour was electorally weak in most of the new areas of industrial and urban expansion, while in the burgeoning suburban areas which clustered around all large cities it made similarly little headway. Despite Labour's progressive rhetoric, its areas of strength were those being left behind by development, not the new and the modern areas themselves.

Labour's urban identification also proved problematic because of the bureaucratic compromise it had developed. Early traditions of municipal socialism had been informed by ideas of local democracy and empowerment. Following the defeat of Poplarism, however, Labour came to endorse a form of bureaucratic welfarism which constructed its working-class electors as passive consumers of municipal beneficence. Morrison himself repudiated the traditional hostility of Labour councillors to council officials (manifested in their frequent support for motions that salaries of council officers should be cut) and deferred willingly to professional expertise. Consequently, it was Labour councils which frequently presided over the development of bureaucratic welfare provision. Local authorities allocated people to council estates after extensive scrutiny of their personal lives and circumstances, and surrounded their tenure with a mass of petty restrictions which emphasised the subservience of tenants to the 'corporation'. Many council estates were built without the social facilities – pubs, shops, markets, churches, libraries – that had existed in more central urban sites, and that helped workers to sustain a vigorous social life. The birth of every child led to endless visits by health visitors and constant checks that mothers were able to look after their babies properly, while Juvenile Employment Bureaux ensured that children's futures were guided and noted once they had left school. This sort of intrusive bureaucratic regime was all too familiar to many people as a result of the introduction of the means test which allowed investigators to evaluate the personal lives of claimants.

The lesson which working-class electors learnt was that the price for much-valued and needed welfare support was bureaucratic intrusiveness and popular passivity to professional expertise. This was a price which many of those in dire straits were willing to pay, but the long-term consequence was to reduce the emotional attachment of many working-class people to the Labour Party. It was precisely this senti-ment that the researchers who wrote *Coal is Our Life* encountered in their study of a post-war mining village.

CONCLUSIONS

In this chapter we have shown that the rise of the Labour Party was not a simple matter of steady progress to a preordained end. Its emergence was halting and unsteady, and at key moments in the course of its development it took directions which had not been foreseen at the outset. We have identified a number of ways in which the Labour Party drew upon the processes of class formation to buttress its unstable electoral support. First, the Labour Party originated as a response to – but ironically as also a contributor to – the bureaucratisation of the labour market. It was the product of a trade union movement, led by skilled male workers, which was all too aware of the fact that it could not avoid formal political activity if it was to retain some measure of control over the labour market. Alongside this shift was a second crucial development: the steady trend towards the unification of the working class. This trend was to have particular repercussions in the immediate post-war period, when great numbers of workers united over trade union demands defending their interests. But we have also argued that this industrial mobilisation did not prove to be a robust electoral base for the Labour Party. It did not address the needs of new female voters, while the defeat and decline of unions in the 1920s forced Labour to look to alternative bases of support. It is for this reason that we have attached particular importance to the urban dimension of Labour's expansion. As the Labour Party met a series of electoral stumbling blocks in the mid-1920s and 1930s it attempted to construct a distinct bloc of supporters in the large industrial cities. This was the crucial period in which the Party succeeded in establishing a secure territorial base, although ultimately, and somewhat ironically, this was a process which was to advance at the expense of popular political participation in Labour politics.

In Chapter 1 we discussed rival interpretations of working-class history. The findings of this book suggest that the principal weaknesses of most of these is their tendency to 'essentialise' the working class. Labour historians perceive the working class as represented through the institutions of the Labour movement, ignoring other working-class practices and attitudes. For the social historians the 'real' working class was the heroic, radical class discerned by E.P. Thompson. The remak-ing of the working class was seen as a process of deradicalisation.

Historians influenced by the 'linguistic turn' deny that the working class existed since it did not use a proper (real) 'language of class'. In this book we have emphasised that the stable monolithic working class suggested by such ideas has never existed. The working class is constantly being made and remade, and the political implications of class formation are often ambiguous and uncertain. This having been said, in the first three decades of the twentieth century the working class developed an unprecedented social and political presence in British society. Although politicians and commentators alike are wont to stress the declining salience of class in our own times, we should be cautious about projecting current scepticism back onto the historical record. Moreover, although the particular working class whose development we have examined in this book may today be undergoing a further process of re-making, this does not constitute an adequate basis for questioning the continued significance of class in general. For so long as we live in an unequal society, in which some people exploit others, class divisions are likely to have profound political ramifications.

Bibliography

Abel-Smith, B. and Townsend, P. (1965), *The Poor and the Poorest*, London: Bell and Sons.

Abercrombie, N. and Warde, A. (1986), *Contemporary British Society*, Oxford: Polity.

Abrams, P. (1982), *Historical Sociology*, Shepton Mallet: Open Books.

Adams, T. (1990), 'Labour and the First World War: Economy, Politics and the Erosion of Local Peculiarity?', *Journal of Local and Regional Studies*, 10, 1, 23–47.

Anderson, M. (1971), *Family Structure in Nineteenth-Century Lancashire*, London: Cambridge University Press.

Anderson, P. (1963), 'Origins of the Present Crisis', *New Left Review*, 23, 26–54.

Bagwell, P. (1963), *The Railwaymen*, London: George Allen and Unwin.

Bealey, F. and Pelling, H. (1958), *Labour and Politics 1900–1906*, London: Macmillan.

Benson, J. (1989), *The Working Class in England 1870–1939*, London: Longman.

Berg, M. and Hudson, P. (1992), 'Rehabilitating the Industrial Revolution', *Economic History Review*, XLV, 1, 24–50.

Bhaskar, R. (1989), *Reality Reclaimed*, London: Verso.

Biagini, E. (1992), *Liberty, Retrenchment and Reform; Popular Liberalism in the Age of Gladstone 1860–1880*, Cambridge: Cambridge University Press.

Biagini, E. and Reid, A. (eds) (1991), *Currents of Radicalism*, Cambridge: Cambridge University Press.

Borsay, P. (1989), *The English Urban Renaissance*, Oxford: Clarendon.

Bradley, H. (1989), *Men's Work, Women's Work*, Oxford: Polity.

Braverman, H. (1974), *Labour and Monopoly Capital*, London: Monthly Review Press.

Braybon, G. (1980), *Women Workers in the First World War*, London: Croom Helm.

Brueilly, M. (1992), *Labour and Liberalism in 19th Century Europe: Essays in Comparative History*, Manchester: Manchester University Press.

Buck, N. (1981), 'The Analysis of State Intervention in 19th Century Cities: the Case of Municipal Labour Policy in East London', in M. Dear and N. Scott (eds), *Urbanisation and Urban Planning in a Capitalist Society*, London: Methuen.

Burgess, K. (1980), *The Challenge of Labour*, London: Croom Helm.

Burgess, K. (1985), 'New Unionism for Old? The Amalgamated Society of Engineers in Britain', in W.J. Mommsen and H.-G. Husung (eds), *The Development of Trade Unionism in Great Britain and Germany, 1880–1914*, London: George Allen and Unwin.

Cain, P.J. and Hopkins, A.G. (1986), 'Gentlemanly Capitalism and British Expansion Overseas 1: the Old Colonial System, 1688–1850', *Economic History Review*, XXXIX, 501–525.

Cain, P.J. and Hopkins, A.G. (1993), *British Imperialism* (2 vols), London: Longman.

Calhoun, C. (1982), *The Question of Class Struggle*, Oxford: Blackwells.

Carr-Saunders, A.M. (1938), *Consumers Co-operation in Great Britain*, Manchester: Co–Op Society.

Chandler, A.D. (1990), *Scale and Scope: The Dynamics of Industrial Capitalism*, Cambridge, Mass.: Harvard University Press

Childs, M.J. (1987), 'Boy Labour in Late Victorian and Edwardian England and the Remaking of the Working Class', *Journal of Social History*, 23, 4, 783–802.

Chinn, C. (1988), *They Worked All Their Lives: Women of the Urban Poor in England, 1880–1939*, Manchester: Manchester University Press.

Clapham, J. (1930), *An Economic History of Modern Britain: the Early Railway Age 1820–1850*, Cambridge: Cambridge University Press.

Clarke, P.F. (1971), *Lancashire and the New Liberalism*, Cambridge: Cambridge University Press.

Cockburn, C. (1980), *Brothers: Male Dominance and Technological Change*, London: Pluto.

Cole, G.D.H. (1948), *A Short History of the British Working-Class Movement 1789–1947*, London: George Allen and Unwin.

Cook, C. (1975), 'Liberals, Labour and Local Elections', in G. Peele and C. Cook (eds), *The Politics of Reappraisal 1918–1939*, London: Macmillan.

Corfield, P. (1982), *The Impact of English Towns*, Oxford: Oxford University Press.

Cornford, J. (1963), 'The Transformation of Conservatism in the Late Nineteenth Century', *Victorian Studies*, 7, 35–66.

Cronin, J.E. (1979), *Industrial Conflict in Modern Britain*, London: Croom Helm.

Cronin, J.E. (1984), *Labour and Society in Britain 1918–1979*, London: Batsford.

Crossick, G. (1978), *An Artisan Elite in Victorian Society*, London: Croom Helm.

Daniel, G. (1939), 'Labour Migration and Age Composition', *Sociological Review*.

Daunton, M. (1977), *Coal Metropolis: Cardiff, 1870–1914*, Leicester: Leicester University Press.

Daunton, M. (1989), '"Gentlemanly Capitalism" and British Industry', *Past and Present*, 122, 119–158.

Davidoff, L. and Hall, C. (1987), *Family Fortunes: Men and Women of the English Middle Class*, London: Methuen.

Davies, A. (1992), *Leisure, Gender and Poverty: Working-class Culture in Salford and Manchester, 1900–1939*, Buckingham: Open University Press.

Dennis, R. (1984), *English Industrial Cities of the Nineteenth Century*, Cambridge: Cambridge University Press.

Dennis, N., Henriques, F. and Slaughter, C. (1969), *Coal is Our Life*, London: Tavistock.

Dews, P. (1987), *Logics of Disintegration: Post-Structuralist Thought and the Claims of Critical Theory*, London: Verso.

Dickens, P., Duncan S., Goodwin, M. and Gray, F. (1985), *Housing, States and Localities*, London: Methuen.

Dintenfass, M. (1992), *The Decline of Industrial Britain 1870–1980*, London: Routledge.

Donoughue, B. and Jones, G.W. (1973), *Herbert Morrison: Portrait of a Politician*, London: Weidenfeld and Nicolson.

Elbaum, W. and Lazonick, W. (1986), *The Decline of the British Economy*, Cambridge: Cambridge University Press.

Engels, F. (1969), *The Condition of the Working Class in England in 1844*, London: Panther.

Farnie, D. (1979), *The English Cotton Industry and the World Market 1815–1896*, Oxford: Clarendon.

Fielding, S. (1993), *Class and Ethnicity*, Buckingham: Open University Press.

Foreman-Peck, J. (1985), 'Seedcorn or Chaff? New Firm Formation and the Performance of the Inter-war Economy', *Economic History Review*, 38, 3, 402–422.

Foster, J. (1974), *Class Struggle in the Industrial Revolution*, London: Methuen.

Franklin, M. (1985), *The Decline of Class Voting in Britain*, Oxford: Clarendon.

Gallie, D. (ed.) (1988), *Employment in Britain*, Oxford: Blackwell.

Garrard, J. (1983), *Leadership and Power in Victorian Industrial Towns, 1830–1880*, Manchester: Manchester University Press.

Garside, P.L., (1990), 'London and the Home Counties', in F.M.L. Thompson (ed.) *The Cambridge Social History of Britain 1750–1950*, Vol.1, Cambridge: Cambridge University Press

Giddens, A. (1984), *The Constitution of Society*, Oxford: Polity.

Ginsberg, M. (1929), 'Interchange between Social Classes', *Economic Journal*, XXXIX, 554–565.

Glass, D.V. (ed.) (1954), *Social Mobility in Britain*, London: Routledge.

Glucksmann, M. (1990), *Women Assemble*, London: Routledge.

Goldthorpe, J.H. (1980), *Social Mobility and Class Structure in Modern Britain*, Oxford: Clarendon.

Goldthorpe, J.H. (1984), 'Women and Class Analysis: a Reply to the Replies', *Sociology*, 18, 491–499.

Goldthorpe J.H. (1987), *Social Mobility and Class Structure in Modern Britain*, Oxford: Clarendon (2nd revised and enlarged edition).

Goldthorpe, J.H. and Lockwood, D. (1969), *The Affluent Worker in the Class Structure*, Cambridge: Cambridge University Press.

Gray, R. (1976), *The Labour Aristocracy in Mid-Victorian Edinburgh*, Oxford: Clarendon.

Gray, R. (1981), *The Aristocracy of Labour in Nineteenth Century Britain*, London: Macmillan.

Gunn, S. (1988), 'The "Failure" of the Victorian Middle Class: a Critique', in J. Wolff and J. Seed (eds), *The Culture of Capital. Art, Power and the*

Nineteenth-Century Middle Class, Manchester: Manchester University Press.

Hall, S. (1983), 'The Great Moving Right Show', in S. Hall and M. Jacques (eds), *The Politics of Thatcherism*, London: Verso.

Hammond, J.L. and Hammond, B. (1917), *The Town Labourer 1760–1832*, London: Longmans.

Hannah, L. (1976), *The Rise of the Corporate Economy*, London: Methuen.

Hannam, J. (1992), 'Women and the ILP, 1890–1914', in D. James, T. Jowitt and K. Laybourn (eds), *The Centennial History of the Independent Labour Party*, Halifax: Ryburn.

Harrison, R. and Zeitlin, J. (1985), *Divisions of Labour*, Brighton: Harvester.

Heath, A. (1981), *Social Mobility*, London: Fontana.

Hennock, E.P (1973), *Fit and Proper Persons: Ideal and Reality in Nineteenth Century Urban Government*, London: Edward Arnold.

Hindess, B. (1987), *Politics and Class Analysis*, Oxford: Blackwells.

Hinton. J. (1973), *The First Shop Stewards' Movement*, London: George Allen and Unwin.

Hinton, J. (1983), *Labour and Socialism*, Brighton: Harvester.

Hobsbawm, E.J. (1964), *Labouring Men*, London: Weidenfeld.

Hobsbawm, E.J. (1981), 'The Forward March of Labour Halted?', in M. Jacques and F. Mulhern (eds), *The Forward March of Labour Halted*, London: New Left Books in association with *Marxism Today*.

Hobsbawm, E.J. (1984), 'The Making of the Working Class 1870–1914' in his *Worlds of Labour*, London: Weidenfeld and Nicolson.

Hobsbawm, E.J. (1985), 'The "New Unionism" Reconsidered', in W.J. Mommsen and H.-G. Husung (eds), *The Development of Trade Unionism in Great Britain and Germany, 1880–1914*, London: George Allen and Unwin.

Hobsbawm, E. (1987), 'Labour in the Great City', *New Left Review*, 166, 39–51.

Hoggart, R. (1957), *The Uses of Literacy*, London: Chatto and Windus.

Holton, B. (1976), *British Syndicalism, 1900–1914*, London: Pluto Press.

Howard, C. (1983), 'Expectations Born unto Death: Local Labour Party Expansion in the 1920s', in J. Winter (ed.), *The Working Class in Modern British Politics*, Cambridge: Cambridge University Press.

Howell, D. (1983), *British Workers and the Independent Labour Party 1888–1906*, Manchester: Manchester University Press.

Howkins, A. (1981), *Poor Labouring Men*, London: Routledge.

Ingham, G. (1986), *Capitalism Divided*, London: Macmillan.

James, D., Jowitt, R. and Laybourn, K. (1992), *The Centennial History of the Independent Labour Party*, Halifax: Ryburn.

Jewkes, J. and Jewkes, S. (1938), *The Juvenile Labour Market*, London: Gollancz.

Johnson, P. (1985), *Saving and Spending. The Working-Class Economy in Britain 1870–1939*, Oxford: Clarendon.

Jowitt. J.A. (ed.) (1986), *Model Industrial Communities in Mid-Nineteenth Century Yorkshire*, Bradford: University of Bradford.

Jowitt, J.A. (1992), 'Late Victorian and Edwardian Bradford', in D. James, T. Jowitt and K. Laybourn (eds), *The Centennial History of the Independent Labour Party*, Halifax: Ryburn.

Joyce, P. (1980), *Work, Society and Politics*, Brighton: Harvester.

Joyce, P. (1990), *Visions of the People*, Cambridge: Cambridge University Press.

Kaye, H.J. (1982), *The British Marxist Historians*, Oxford: Polity.

Kingsford, P.W. (1970), *Victorian Railwaymen*, London: Cass.

Kirk, N. (1985), *The Growth of Working Class Reformism in Mid-Victorian England*, London: Croom Helm.

Kumar, K. (1978), *Prophecy and Progress*, Harmondsworth: Penguin.

Lambertz, J. (1985), 'Sexual Harassment in the Cotton Industry', *History Workshop Journal*, 19, 29–61.

Lancaster, B. (1987), *Radicalism, Co-operation and Socialism: Leicester Working Class Politics 1860–1906*, Leicester: Leicester University Press.

Lash, S. and Urry, J. (1987), *The End of Organized Capitalism*, Oxford: Polity.

Lawrence, J. (1991), 'Popular Politics and the Limitations of Party: Wolverhampton; 1867–1900', in Biagini and Reid (1991), 65–85.

Laybourn, K. (1992), 'Recent Writing on the History of the ILP', in D. James, T. Jowitt and K. Laybourn (eds), *The Centennial History of the Independent Labour Party*, Halifax: Ryburn.

Lazonick, W. (1979), 'Industrial Relations and Technical Change: the Case of the Self-acting Mule', *Cambridge Journal of Economics*, 3, 231–262.

Lazonick, W. (1983), 'Industrial Organisation and Technological Change: the Decline of the British Cotton Industry', *Business History Review*, CVIII.

Lee, C. (1981), 'Regional Growth and Structural Change in Victorian Britain', *Economic History Review*, 33, 438–452.

Lee, C.H. (1979), *Regional Employment Statistics, 1841–1971*, Cambridge: Cambridge University Press.

Lewis, J. (1984), *Women in England 1870–1950*, Brighton: Wheatsheaf.

Liddington, J. and Norris, J. (1978), *One Hand Tied Behind Us*, London: Virago.

Littler, C. (1982), *The Transformation of the Labour Process in Capitalist Societies*, London: Heinemann.

Lockwood, D. (1958), *The Blackcoated Worker: a Study in Class Consciousness*, Oxford: Clarendon.

Lockwood, D. (1988), 'The Weakest Link in the Chain: Some Remarks on the Marxist Theory of Action', in D. Rose (ed.), *Social Stratification and Economic Change*, London: Hutchinson.

McKenna, F. (1980), *The Railway Worker*, London: Faber.

McKibbin, R. (1975), *The Evolution of the Labour Party, 1910–1924*, London: Oxford University Press.

McKibbin, R. (1990), *The Ideologies of Class*, Oxford: Clarendon.

McKinlay, A. and Morris, R.J. (eds) (1991), *The ILP on Clydeside 1893–1932: from Foundation to Disintegration*, Manchester: Manchester University Press.

MacLean, I. (1983), *The Legend of Red Clydeside*, Edinburgh: John Donald.

McLelland, K. (1987), 'Time to Work, Time to Live: Some Aspects of Work and the Reformation of Class in Britain, 1850–1880', in P. Joyce (ed.), *The Historical Meanings of Work*, Cambridge: Cambridge University Press.

McLelland, K. and Reid, A. (1985), 'Wood, Iron and Steel: Technology, Labour and Trade Union Organisation in the Shipbuilding Industry, 1840–1914', in Harrison and Zeitlin (1995).

McLeod, H. (1974), *Religion and Class in the Victorian City*, London: Croom Helm.

Mark-Lawson, J. and Witz, A. (1988), 'From "Family Labour" to "Family Wage"? The Case of Women's Labour in Nineteenth Century Coalmining', *Social History*, 13, 2, 151–174.

Mark-Lawson, J., Savage, M. and Warde, A. (1985), 'Gender and Local Politics: Struggles over Welfare 1918–1939', in L. Murgatroyd, M. Savage, D. Shapiro, J. Urry, S. Walby and A. Warde, *Localities, Class and Gender*, London: Pion.

Matthew, H., McKibbin, R. and Kay, J. (1976), 'The Franchise Factor in the Rise of the Labour Party', *English Historical Review*, CCCLXI, 723–752.

Meacham, S. (1977), *A Life Apart. The English Working Class, 1890–1914*, London: Thames and Hudson.

Melling, J. (1980), '"Non-commissioned Officers": British Employers and Their Supervisory Workers, 1880–1920', *Social History*, 5, 183–221.

Melling, J. (1983), *Rent Strikes. People's Struggle for Housing in West Scotland 1890–1916*, Edinburgh: Polygon.

Miles, A.G. (1992), 'Occupational and Social Mobility in England, 1830–1914', PhD thesis, Keele University.

Miles, A.G. (1993a), 'How Open was Nineteenth Century British Society? Social Mobility and Equality of Opportunity, 1839–1914', in Miles and Vincent (1993).

Miles, A.G. (1993b), 'Lower-Middle Class Mobility in England, 1839–1914', *Bulletin de Centre Piere Leon*, Autumn.

Miles, A.G. (1993c), 'Calculating the Career: Careers and Social Mobility in Britain 1840–1940', mimeo.

Miles, A.G. and Vincent, D. (eds) (1993), *Building European Society: Occupational and Social Mobility in Europe, 1840–1940*, Manchester: Manchester University Press.

Miliband, R. (1961), *Parliamentary Socialism*, London: Allen and Unwin.

Mitch, D. (1993), '"Inequalities Which Everyone May Remove": Occupational Recruitment, Endogamy, and the Homogeneity of Social Origins in Victorian England', in Miles and Vincent (1993).

Moorhouse, H.F. (1978), 'The Marxist Theory of the Labour Aristocracy', *Social History*, 3, 1, 61–82.

More, C. (1980), *Skill and the English Working Class*, London: Croom Helm.

Morris, R.J. (1983), 'The Middle Class and British Towns and Cities of the Industrial Revolution 1780–1870', in D. Fraser and A. Sutcliffe (eds), *The Pursuit of Urban History*, London: Edward Arnold.

Morris, R.J. (1990), *Class, Sect and Party: the Making of the British Middle Classes: Leeds 1820–1850*, Manchester: Manchester University Press.

Musson, A.E. (1954), *The Typographical Association*, London: Oxford University Press.

Musson, A.E. (1978), *The Growth of British Industry*, London: Batsford.

Nairn, T. (1964a), 'The English Working Class', *New Left Review*, 24, 43–57.

Nairn, T. (1964b), 'The Nature of the Labour Party' (2 parts), *New Left Review*, 27, 38–65 and 28, 33–62.

Owen, A.D.K. (1937), 'The Social Consequences of Industrial Transference', *Sociological Review*, XXIX, 331–354.

Pahl, R.E. (1984), *Divisions of Labour*, Oxford: Blackwell.

Pelling, H. (1965), *The Origins of the Labour Party*, Oxford: Clarendon Press.

Pelling, H. (1968), *Popular Politics and Society in Late Victorian Britain*, London: Macmillan.

Penn, R. (1983), 'The Course of Wage Differentials between Skilled and Nonskilled Manual Workers in Britain between 1856 and 1864', *British Journal of Industrial Relations*, XXI, 1, 69–90.

Penn, R. (1985), *Skilled Manual Workers in the Class Structure*, Cambridge: Cambridge University Press.

Phillips, G. and Whiteside N. (1985), *Casual Labour: The Unemployment Question in the Port Industry*, Oxford: Clarendon Press.

Pollard, S. (1959), *A History of Labour in Sheffield*, Liverpool: Liverpool University Press.

Pooley, C. (1979), 'Residential Mobility in the Victorian City', *Transactions of the Institute of British Geographers*, NS 4, 258–277.

Pooley, C. and Irish, S. (1987), 'Access to Housing on Merseyside, 1919–1939', *Transactions of the Institute of British Geographers*, NS 12, 177–191.

Price, R. (1980), *Masters, Unions and Men: Work Control in Building and the Rise of Labour*, Cambridge: Cambridge University Press.

Price, R. (1985), 'The New Unionism and the Labour Process', in W.J. Mommsen and H.-G. Husung, *The Development of Trade Unionism in Great Britain and Germany, 1880–1914*, London: George Allen and Unwin.

Price, R. (1986), *Labour in British Society*, London: Croom Helm.

Prothero, I. (1979), *Artisans and Politics: the Life and Times of John Gast*, Folkestone: Dawson.

Pugh, M. (1985), *The Tories and the People 1880–1935*, Oxford: Blackwell.

Purvis, M. (1990), 'The Development of Co-operative Retailing in England and Wales, 1851–1901: a Geographical Study', *Journal of Historical Geography*, 16, 3, 314–331.

Reddy, W. (1987), *Money and Liberty in Western Europe*, Cambridge: Cambridge University Press.

Reid, A. (1978), 'Politics and Economics in the Formation of the British Working Class: a Response to Moorhouse', *Social History*, 3, 3, 347–362.

Reid, A. (1980), 'The Division of Labour in the British Shipbuilding Industry, 1880–1920', PhD thesis, Cambridge University.

Reid, A. (1985), 'Politics and the Division of Labour 1880–1920', in H.J. Mommsen and H.-G. Husung (eds) *The Development of Trade Unionism in Britain and Germany*, London: George Allen and Sons.

Reid, A. (1991), 'Old Unionism Reconsidered: the Radicalism of Robert Knight, 1870–1900', in Biagini and Reid (1991).

Reid, A. (1992), *Social Classes and Social Relations in Britain, 1850–1914*, London: Macmillan.

Reynolds, J. (1983), *The Great Paternalist*, Hounslow: Maurice Temple Smith in association with the University of Bradford.

Roberts, E. (1984), *A Woman's Place. An Oral History of Working-Class Women 1890–1940*, Oxford: Blackwell.

Roberts, R. (1973), *The Classic Slum. Salford Life in the First Quarter of the Century*, Harmondsworth: Penguin.

Rose, G. (1989), 'Locality Studies and Waged Labour: an Historical Critique', *Transactions of the Institute of British Geographers*, 3, 317–328.

Ross, E. (1983), 'Survival Networks: Womens' Neighbourhood Sharing before World War 1', *History Workshop Journal*, 15, 4–27.

Routh, G. (1980), *Occupation and Pay in Great Britain 1906–1979*, London: Macmillan.

Rubinstein, W. (1981), *Men of Property*, London: Croom Helm.

Rubinstein, W. (1987), 'The Geographical Distribution of Middle Class Income in Britain 1800–1914', in his *Elites and the Wealthy in Modern British History*, Brighton: Harvester.

Rule, J. (1986), *The Labouring Classes in Early Industrial England, 1750–1850*, London: Longman.

Samuel, R. (1977), 'The Workshop of the World: Steam Power and Hand Technology in mid-Victorian Britain', *History Workshop Journal*, 3, 6–72.

Sanderson, M. (1972), 'Literacy and Social Mobility in the Industrial Revolution in England', *Past and Present*, 56, 75–104.

Saunders, P. (1990), *A Nation of Homeowners*, London: Unwin Hyman.

Savage, M. (1985), 'Capitalist and Patriarchal Relations at Work: Preston Cotton Weaving', in L. Murgatroyd, M. Savage, D. Shapiro, J. Urry, S. Walby and A. Warde, *Localities, Class and Gender*, London: Pion.

Savage, M. (1987), *The Dynamics of Working Class Politics: the Labour Movement in Preston 1880–1914*, Cambridge: Cambridge University Press.

Savage. M. (1988a), 'Women and Work in the Lancashire Cotton Industry, 1890–1939', in J.A. Jowitt and A.J. McIvor (eds), *Employers and Labour in the English Textile Industries*, London: Routledge.

Savage, M. (1988b), 'Trade Unionism, Sex Segregation and the State: Women's Employment in "New Industries" in Inter-war Britain', *Social History*, 13, 2, 209–230.

Savage, M. (1990), 'Urban Politics and the Rise of the Labour Party 1919–1939', in L. Jamieson and H. Corr (eds), *State, Private Life and Political Change*, Basingstoke: Macmillan.

Savage, M. (1993a), 'Career, Mobility and Class Formation: British Banking Workers and the Lower Middle Classes', in Miles and Vincent (1993).

Savage, M. (1993b), 'Discipline and the Construction of the Modern Career: the Case of the Great Western Railway 1850–1920', mimeo.

Savage, M. (1994), 'Social Mobility and Class Analysis: A New Agenda for Social Historians?', *Social History*, 19, 1, 69–79.

Savage, M., Barlow, J., Dickens, P. and Fielding, A.J. (1992), *Property, Bureaucracy and Culture: Middle Class Formation in Contemporary Britain*, London: Routledge.

Scott, J. (1988), 'Ownership and Employer Control' in D. Gallie (ed.), *Employment in Britain*, Oxford: Blackwell.

Sewell, W.H. (1985), *Structure and Mobility. The Men and Women of Marseilles*, Cambridge: Cambridge University Press.

Shepherd, M. and Halstead, J. (1979), 'Labour's Municipal Election Performance in Provincial England and Wales 1900–1913', *Bulletin of the Society for the Study of Labour History*, 45.

Sjoberg, G. (1960), *The Pre-Industrial City: Past and Present*, New York: Free Press.

Smith, D. (1982), *Conflict and Compromise: Class Formation in English Society 1830–1914*, London: Routledge.

Smith, J. (1984), 'Labour Tradition in Glasgow and Liverpool', *History Workshop Journal*, 17, 32–56.

Smyth, J.J. (1991), 'The ILP in Glasgow, 1888–1906: the Struggle for Identity', in McKinlay and Morris (1991).

Southall, H. (1991), 'The Tramping Artisan Revisits: Labour Mobility and Economic Distress in Early Victorian England', *Economic History Review*, XLIV, 2, 272–296.

Stedman Jones, G. (1971), *Outcast London*, Harmondsworth: Penguin.

Stedman Jones, G. (1974), 'Working Class Culture and Working Class Politics in London 1870–1900: Notes on the Remaking of a Working Class', *Journal of Social History*, 7, 4 (reprinted in Stedman Jones 1983).

Stedman Jones, G. (1975), 'Class Struggle and the Industrial Revolution', *New Left Review*, 90, 35–69.

Stedman Jones, G. (1983), *Languages of Class*, Cambridge: Cambridge University Press.

Stedman Jones, G. (1984), *Outcast London*, Harmondsworth: Penguin, 2nd edition.

Stevenson, J. (1984), *British Society, 1914–45*, Harmondsworth: Penguin.

Stevenson, J. and Cook, C. (1979), *The Slump: Politics and Society in the Great Depression*, London: Quartet.

Stinchcombe, A. (1959), 'Bureaucratic and Craft Administration of Production: a Comparative Study', *Administrative Science Quarterly*, 4, 168–187.

Tanner, D. (1990), *Political Change and the Labour Party*, Cambridge: Cambridge University Press.

Taylor, B. (1983), '"The Men are as Bad as their Masters . . ." Socialism, Feminism and Sexual Antagonism in the London Tailoring Trade in the 1830s', in J.L. Newton, M.P. Ryan and J.R. Walkowitz (eds), *Sex and Class in Women's History*, London: Routledge.

Thane, P. (1985), 'The Labour Party and State "Welfare"', in K.D. Brown (ed.), *The First Labour Party 1906–1910*, London: Croom Helm.

Thane, P. (1991), 'Labour and Local Politics: Radicalism, Democracy and Social Reform', in Biagini and Reid (1991).

Thompson, D. (1984), *The Chartists*, London: Temple Smith.

Thompson, E.P. (1955), *William Morris, Romantic to Revolutionary*, London: Merlin.

Thompson, E.P. (1961), 'Homage to Tom Maguire', in A. Briggs and J. Saville (eds), *Essays in Labour History*, London: Macmillan.

Thompson, E.P. (1965), 'The Peculiarities of the English', *Socialist Register*, 2, 311–362 (reprinted in Thompson 1978).

Thompson, E.P. (1968), *The Making of the English Working Class*, Harmondsworth: Penguin.

Thompson, E.P. (1978), *The Poverty of Theory*, London: Merlin.

Treble, J. (1979), *Urban Poverty in Britain, 1830–1914*, London: Batsford.

Turner, H.A. (1962), *Trade Union Growth, Structure and Policy. A Comparative Study of the Cotton Unions*, London: George Allen and Unwin.

Vincent, D. (1989), *Literacy and Popular Culture. England 1750–1914*, Cambridge: Cambridge University Press.

Vincent, D. (1991), *Poor Citizens. The State and the Poor in Twentieth-Century Britain*, London: Longman.

Vincent, D. (1993), 'Mobility, Bureaucracy and Careers in Early Twentieth Century Britain', in Miles and Vincent (1993).

Waites, B. (1987), *A Class Society at War. England 1914–18*, Leamington Spa: Berg.

Walby, S. (1986), *Patriarchy at Work*, Oxford: Polity.

Walkowitz, J. (1992), *City of Dreadful Delight*, London: Virago.

Waller, P.J. (1983), *Town, City and Nation. England 1850–1914*, Oxford: Oxford University Press.

Ward, D. (1975), 'Victorian Cities: How Modern?', *Journal of Historical Geography*, 1, 2, 135–151.

Webb, B. and Webb, S. (1902), *Industrial Democracy*, London: Longman.

Weiner, M.J. (1981), *English Culture and the Decline of the Industrial Spirit, 1850–1980*, Cambridge: Cambridge University Press.

White, J.L. (1986), *The Worst Street in North London: Campbell Bunk, Islington, Between the Wars*, London: Routledge.

Wild, P. (1979), 'Recreation in Rochdale 1900–1940', in J. Clarke, C. Critcher and R. Johnson (eds), *Working Class Culture*, London: Hutchinson.

Wright, E.O. (1978), *Class, Crisis and the State*, London: Verso.

Wright, E.O. (1985), *Classes*, London: Verso.

Zeitlin, J. (1979), 'Craft Control and the Division of Labour: Engineers and Compositors in Britain 1880–1930', *Cambridge Journal of Economics*, 3 (September), 263–274.

Zeitlin, J. (1980), 'The Emergence of Shop Steward Organisation and Job Control in the British Car Industry', *History Workshop Journal*, 10, 119–137.

Zeitlin, J. (1985), 'Industrial Structure, Employer Strategy and the Diffusion of Job Control in Britain, 1850–1920' in H.J. Mommsen and H.-G. Husung (eds) *The Development of Trade Unionism in Britain and Germany 1880–1914*, London: George Allen and Unwin.

Name index

Place and subject index